Tone Deaf and All Thumbs?

Tone Deaf AND *All Thumbs?*

AN INVITATION TO MUSIC-MAKING

Frank R. Wilson

VINTAGE BOOKS
A DIVISION OF RANDOM HOUSE
NEW YORK

For
Pat, Jeff, Suzanna, and Ma
and
in memory of Eloise Ristad.
This book is for her and,
in a very real sense, from her.

First Vintage Books Edition, November 1987

 Published in the United States by Random House, Inc., New York, and simultaneously in Canada by Random House of Canada Limited, Toronto. Originally published, in hardcover, by Viking Penguin, Inc., in 1986.

Library of Congress Cataloging-in-Publication Data
Wilson, Frank R.
Tone deaf and all thumbs?
Includes bibliographies.
1. Music—Physiological aspects. 2. Neurology.
I. Title.
[ML3820.W56 1987] 781'.15 87-40086
ISBN 0-394-75354-2 (pbk.)

Grateful acknowledgment is made for permission to reprint the following copyrighted material: Excerpt from "Adelaide's Lament" by Frank Loesser from *Guys and Dolls*.
 Letter to the author from Dr. Mac McRobbie.

DISPLAY TYPOGRAPHY BY WENDY KASSNER

Manufactured in the United States of America
10 9 8 7 6 5 4

Acknowledgments

The assembly of a book whose origins are as diverse and peculiar as is the case here leaves its author in something of a quandary. It is not merely a question of finding the words to thank all those who nudged or dragged you along, sparked a synapse, shared their pearls of wisdom, brought coffee (or something stronger), or warned you away from the quicksand. How can you fail to neglect the importance of a chance remark, a simple word of encouragement, an effort on your behalf made out of your view—the gift by *anon.* I think you can do very little beyond hoping your message of gratitude lands where it should. In that spirit, thanks beyond measure go out, as follows:

To Lillian Bauer Cox, my piano teacher for five years, who lavished her love of music on a late-blooming nonprodigy (and his daughter and his wife), and launched a new career with a request to teach her other students something about the brain.

To the memory of Carl Coleman, my high school band teacher, who loved kids, music, work, and play.

To the memory of Eloise Ristad, a woman of boundless energy, warmth, and good humor, who had the personal clarity and strength one finds only in people in love with life and their work, and who know what they are doing. As a teacher, hers was the happiest of missions: to awaken (or revive) in musicians a passion for play. She knew that an artist free enough to be childlike would come to understand how music can bring people together in a celebration of life.

To David Turner, Jack Meehan, Wayne Downey, Pat Crossen, and Mary Langenberg—our kids were lucky enough to have them as teachers, counselors, and friends, and I was lucky enough to see them in action.

To colleagues in medicine and science who listened to my nonsense, thought it over, then offered enormous amounts of advice, help, and good information: Sid Gilman, Bob Efron, George Moore, Tom Thach, John Brust, Frank Benson, Tedd Judd, John Mazziotta, Elliott Ross, Peter Ostwald, Gary Gelber, Paul Lehrer, and Howard Mel.

To Betty Looney, Dorothy Taubman, and Rita Fuszek, who made it clear that music teachers aren't sitting down and they aren't standing still.

To Margaret Rowell, whose love of learning, of life, of music, and of the cello have made her a beacon among music teachers; Margaret *is* the fountain of youth.

To my friends in the American Music Conference and the Public Relations Board, who made me believe it was important to tell people what music is and whom it is for; especially to Roman Babiak, Betty Stearns, and Tari Marshall, who kept asking when I was going to write a book.

To James Roy at Broadcast Music, Inc., who keeps opening doors.

To Gideon Waldrop at Juilliard and Robert Freeman at Eastman, who believe American audiences haven't yet discovered how good our musicians really are.

To Mariann Clinton, Sigfred Matson, Dolores Zupan, and Frank McGinnis of the Music Teachers National Association, who believe in the future and are willing to bet on it.

To Franz Roehmann and Roy Pritts at the University of Colorado, partners in a larger conspiracy.

To Neal Larrabee, who brought Godzilla (our piano) to life.

To Loren Pedersen, who helped me to dig a little deeper.

To Linda Whalen, secretary and friend, who knows how to

laugh and how to get things done at the same time, and keeps forgetting to collect for the overtime.

To Harry Randall, whose musical sophistication, wit, and literary instincts are in evidence throughout this book.

To Rosalie Siegel, who believed in the book and was willing to put up with my neurotic behavior to see that it got done.

To Amanda Vaill, my editor at Viking, whose literary, musical, and surgical instincts brought the book into the world.

To the many people who have reviewed portions of the manuscript, and especially to Karl Bruhn, Mort Lindsey, and Rosario Mazzeo.

To the Blue Crew, creators of the world's biggest goose bumps.

To the muse of craziness and fun.

And especially to Pat, my wife, who for twenty-six years has made sure there was music in our home, and who sends me flowers.

Contents

Tone Deaf and All Thumbs?

Introduction

When I left college, I began a three-year tour of duty in the Navy aboard an aircraft carrier. Most of my memories of shipboard life are hazy, but some remain fresh and vivid. On one unusually stormy and harrowing night of flight operations, the captain was approached by an anxious and upset flight officer, who wanted to call off the remaining flights because there were no more spare parts for an essential piece of the ship's landing control system. The captain looked icily at this younger officer over a pair of half-mast spectacles, pausing long enough before his reply to signal that he was making a pronouncement: "George, you know perfectly well I don't believe in keeping equipment on the shelf just to have it there. If you've got it, *use* it!"

My purpose in writing this book is to tell you about some of the special equipment *you* have, and to encourage you to find out more about it by using it. In particular, I hope to acquaint you with your inborn ability to make music, which is as much a part of your makeup as the color of your eyes and the amazing ability you have to read what is in front of you at this moment.

It is entirely possible that your musical inclinations are strictly those of the avid listener, and you feel no urge to change. Does this book have anything to offer you? I suspect it might if you find musicians as interesting as their music. Just as the program notes provided by an artist enhance a concert, a guide to the inner workings of the artist could add a fresh and important dimension to your listening experience.

Still, I must warn you: Most of us know very little about our own suppressed fantasies, and I cannot promise you immunity from the encouragement this book is intended to provide the fledgling music-maker. Should you suddenly find yourself overwhelmed by the impulse to take tuba lessons, I wouldn't be surprised and I won't apologize.

Although there is an endless variety of things we can do and enjoy during our lives because of our physical makeup, there is something so distinctive about our musicality that it deserves special notice. Even if you are already a musician, I suspect you will be astonished at what you will read here, and will find it helpful to your development.

For a number of reasons which we will explore in this book, I am convinced that all of us have a biologic guarantee of musicianship. This is true regardless of our age, formal experience with music, or the size and shape of our fingers, lips, or ears. So many musicians are undeterred by blindness, hearing impairment, and strokes that not even physical disability seems much of a barrier. We all have music inside us, and can learn how to get it out, one way or another. We are natural musicians because of the special nature of the human brain and the phenomenal muscular system to which it is attached.

I know there will be objections to the claim that everyone can be a musician, so let me stress what seems to be the simple truth about people's abilities: No two people are the same. Just as there are athletes who can run a mile in less than four minutes and far more who *can't,* there are pianists who can play Chopin's B Minor Sonata and far more who can't. Moreover, it is a mistake to presume that people normally exercise in a maniacal frame of mind, content only with hammering away at their own physiologic limits. There are many whose athletic inclinations are occasionally (or exclusively) of the less arduous kind, who are well satisfied with a low pressure game of tennis, or even a relaxed stroll around the block. Similarly, you can roam happily through an enormous amount of music which will neither break your knuckles nor dislodge your dentures during the first five measures.

No matter what they are attempting to do, however seriously or vigorously, people working at physical (or so-called motor) skills are athletes in training—yes, even guitarists, flute players, and pianists!—and all will experience a growing sense of personal fulfillment as they work to improve their proficiency.

What about talent? You can stop worrying; talent has to do with the degree of success our efforts have with the public. If we please an audience, or the critics, we have talent. So be it. But if we are privately shaping our interests and developing our skills, there is no reason to bother ourselves with the reviews.

In a sense, the recreational musician is far better off than the individual so talented or gifted that music as a livelihood has become a possibility. The sad truth is that our society is not generous to musicians. The performance career is intellectually, physically, and emotionally demanding, and those who succeed have usually worked many years before there is much hope of recognition or financial success. You and I can approach musical training at our leisure and without the extreme pressures faced by professionals.

As you are doubtless aware, libraries bulge with books on music appreciation; what is offered here is perhaps the first attempt to build a base for *musician* appreciation. If you happen to be a musician already, or are eager to try your wings, these pages will provide a slant on the learning experience that could sharpen your focus, stimulate your curiosity, and perhaps boost your resolve when your ego is under fire.

My intent is to present a picture of the brain and muscular system to help you build a specific (rather than a romantic) picture of the body as a natural learner. We will consider the neurologic basis of auditory perception—how we hear, and what is so special about musical hearing. We will also look at the biology of timing, rhythm, and tempo. We will spend some time with the visual system, to try to make sense of the musical notation system and the problems it presents to the brain as a processor of information encoded in light waves. We will consider a few principles of learning theory, particularly as it applies to music. Finally, we will take a look at life in the fast lane: what it's like to be onstage.

In short, we will look at *you* as the repository of innate tendencies and skills which will make you something of a music machine. If you do decide to take the plunge, I cannot predict how far you might go with music, or how fast you will progress, any more than I can predict your personal taste in music or the specific instrument you are most likely to succeed with. You have more than enough native ability to enjoy a lifetime of music-making if you choose to, but it's up to you to decide whether and how to use that capacity.

It has occurred to me more than once that this book might be taken as just another of the current crop about the brain, masquerading as a music book. This is a judgment I would scarcely oppose, unless it was made to quibble about the narrowly skewed output of neurologists writing about the world: "What next? The Brain and Motorcycle Repair, I suppose." The truth is that there is ample room for books about human potential and experience specifically related to concepts of brain function. To the extent that other neurologists are willing to take up the pen to expound their views, you can expect more of this kind of writing in the near future. In fact, a case could be made for having neurologists emulate the dentists' crusade against tooth decay; if we could occasionally pry people (especially children) away from their television sets, we might be doing something to attack one of the causes of *brain* decay. Make no mistake about it, the brain is *not* a sponge; our greatest gift is the capacity for learning, and we learn by actively exploring what is around us. I'm with that Navy captain—leave your brain on the shelf and it will surely turn to pudding.

Music may get you away from the television set once in a while. It may help open the door to new friendships. It may lead you to discover a new way of saying things you need to say. It may even cure warts. Maybe it will just give you the blahs. If it is a remedy for your ills, it is a placebo, nontoxic when approached in the proper spirit, and available as a prescription you can learn to write for yourself.

In case you are undecided about your own interest, you may wish to consider two additional benefits that fell to me as a result of beginning the study of music when it was already "too late." It may also occur to you, as it has to me, that the cultural value or appeal of music need not be abstract, academic, or highbrow. There is nothing like active participation to bring this realization alive.

I recall being told in my early teens that the music of any period reflects something of the society in which it was conceived: Listen to the music of Mozart, or of Chopin, and you immerse yourself in the traditions of an earlier culture. No one would gainsay this special attraction of music—without it symphonic music would hardly be as popular as it is. But something far more personal, and more powerful, occurred as a result of my trying to *play* music that had been written long before I was born.

The first time it happened, I was practicing Debussy's *La Cathédrale Engloutie* (The Sunken Cathedral) when the piano unexpectedly yielded a sound I had neither heard nor even imagined before. I felt almost as though the piano and I were going to float right out the window, that Debussy and I were in the room together, outside of time, suspended in a resonance he had created in his mind when he wrote the piece. I played the chord again several times to make sure my ears hadn't deceived me, then went outside and looked at trees for an hour or so. Music can surprise you this way, making you wonder a bit about the nature of human affinity, or even about our notions of immortality.

Then there is a cultural issue with less mystical connotations, having to do with one of our society's more contemporary concerns; I refer to what is called the generation gap.

Parents and their children rarely share the same interests as peers. As soon as I became personally involved in music, I found myself extremely interested in whatever ideas and advice our kids could give me about my own efforts. I learned quickly that they were capable of being understanding, sympathetic, and even wise, and that they had a great deal to teach me. Our common interest in music has done as much to nourish our rapport as anything else we have ever done as a family, and if one of the kids ever offered me a spot in a combo, I'd be on the next plane.

A final caveat: Some of the material in the book is technical in nature, and you will have to take your time with it. Music can be like that, too. But if you have enough curiosity to ask (and the determination to pursue) the question "I wonder if *I* could do that?" you'll make it. The book is not a magic wand; if you decide to explore your musical side you *will* have to work. My hope is that I will not only encourage you to discover what you can do but also help to make the effort more of the pleasure it can and should be. If you're anything like me, you will throw up your hands, snarl, gnash your teeth, and quit more than once. That's half the fun.

1

Is Music a Physical Culture?

A stocky young genius named Herbie
Whose life was a bore and a mess
Had already "done" roller derby
And he wasn't excited by chess.

He stewed and he sulked and he mumbled
Till his girlfriend, who knew what and how,
Said "Herbie, you need to be humbled—
Buy a banjo! Get going right now!"

In recent years a largely sedentary and listless population has shown a surprising interest in recreational athletics. Although the earmarks of faddishness abound, there are signs that people's attitudes about themselves physically are undergoing genuine and perhaps durable change. It is difficult to imagine anyone being surprised at the sight of a fiftyish man or woman in full running regalia, plodding or dashing along a city street. Indeed, those who do not participate in the physical renaissance are beginning to feel the need to make excuses for their inertia.

This excited awareness of the body's physical potential, and the great popularity of novel approaches to the exploration of that potential, make the time ripe for a new slant on one of our most venerable pastimes—music. At first glance, the notion of the musician as an athlete seems contrived, if not downright comical. By what stretch of the imagination can one consider a violinist even remotely akin to a wrestler? Glad you asked.

Despite the stereotyped and mutually uncomplimentary notions you might encounter in football locker rooms and recital halls, there is surprisingly little to distinguish the serious musician from the serious athlete, apart from this: The musician concentrates on improving control of the small muscles of the upper extremities (mainly the hands) or those of the mouth and the airway (which includes the muscles involved in breathing and vocalizing). Musicians tend to stay put when they're at work, but there are some spectacular exceptions (go to a drum and bugle corps show the next time you have an opportunity). Lastly, musicians keep track of what they're doing by listening to the sounds they are making—they use the auditory system to monitor their output, if you have that kind of vocabulary.

By contrast, whether prized by coach and fans for speed or for impersonating a wall, the athlete develops mainly the trunk, leg, and upper arm muscles. On the sports field, the athlete is usually on the move, hotly pursuing opponents, teammates, or an inanimate object whose ownership, location, or trajectory is a passionate concern from start to finish. Although the athlete listens intently for the sound of unfriendly footsteps at his heel, and longs for the cheers of an adoring crowd, he is mostly in need of a sharp eye to be a successful competitor.

In certain sports, most notably gymnastics and ice skating, and of course in ballet, the striking parallels of these physical disciplines are unobscured. Proficiency and success require, among other things, long periods of repetitious training in which countless hours are spent on drills and exercises which condition muscles and establish patterns and increasingly complex sequences of movements. These must be learned so well that they can be executed whenever needed, almost automatically. When the necessary moves have been mastered to a certain level of expertness, the athlete or performer moves to a sort of summit experience—live performance—during which the effort is made to perform flawlessly.

During a sporting event, the athlete confronts a live competitor whom he must outperform if he is to win the contest. Although the musician is not generally perceived as being in a contest, there are occasions when this is literally the case, and in a concert situation there may be an unseen competitor, a sort of ghost, in the form of another musician who is remembered by the audience or a critic as having set a standard for the music being presented. The serious musician, although usually more concerned with communicating than with winning approval, is just as concerned as his counterpart on the athletic field with the quality of performance, and is equally subject to the effects of performance stress.

In addition to advantages of digital versatility and speed compared to nonmusical brothers or sisters, the musician enjoys the opportunity for increasing refinement and maturation of his or her skills well beyond the age at which even the most durable football or baseball player has retired to the sidelines. Arthur Rubinstein, for example, claimed that he did not really begin to play as he wanted until he was nearly eighty. It's not that hard to keep the chops in shape.*

*I made this statement in a talk at a music conservatory a few years ago, and was hauled up by a student who accused me of playing with the truth. "You don't really think Rubinstein played, or even *thought* he played, better at eighty than he did at fifty, do you?" he challenged. I asked the student what he meant by "played." Certainly the technique had faded somewhat by the ninth decade. But what of the message, and his powers of communication? I reminded my detractor of the famous Watergate hearings in the summer of 1973, during which the late Senator Sam Ervin, who could scarcely stutter and stumble his way through a sentence, so electrified the world with his knowledge, judgment, humor, courage, and humanity that we became embarrassed by the courtroom posturing ("technique") of his young and vapid colleagues.

So much for the champions, athletic and musical. What about the rest of us? As a nation, we are unabashed hero-worshipers. We revere the virtuoso, whatever the *shtick*—the movie star, the Olympic diving champion, the lead guitar in our favorite rock 'n' roll band, and especially the quarterback of our favorite pro football team—and will pay anything to get close enough for the briefest glimpse. We love them for their magic, but until recently assumed we could never do what they do and would never try to. We buy albums and pictures. We are allowed to wear buttons, booster jackets, and funny hats, but *not* the uniform.

Clearly, though, sheepishness over getting outfitted in running shoes, or buying a tennis racket, is on the wane. The average adult is no longer intimidated by the apparent obstacles to physical achievement. For one thing, the risk of ridicule for lack of proficiency is far less than it seemed to be just a few years ago. People have discovered that it's fun to take a swing at a baseball, tennis ball, or golf ball. Not only that, if you work at it you get better.

There is not the slightest doubt in my mind that the rise of the amateur athlete in the past decade has at least three explanations: First, virtually everyone has ample and generally untapped resources for refinement of physical skill; second, people are starved for challenges of any kind, and will pursue them avidly if given the hope of success, *fanatically* if they can have a good time in the process; third, the folks in the sports and advertising industries (who aren't slow or stupid) have made amateur sports not only socially acceptable but glamorous.

Music, for reasons I would like to explore with you, has not been part of this revolution in people's attitudes about fresh air, fitness, fun, and a new waistline. It remains a spectator sport. To the individual who has never studied music, it is mysterious, its practitioners bland and bookish (not counting David Lee Roth and other less determined hedonists), and it is unlearnable.

The mention of Mr. Roth, widely recognized as a tireless champion of the California way of life, brings me to the matter of California parents and their reliance on kids for guidance when there are decisions to be made about the use of leisure time. My personal introduction to music can be accounted for in exactly this way, as proclaimed in the famous quip:

INSANITY IS INHERITED—YOU GET IT FROM YOUR KIDS!

Our daughter began noodling on the piano when she was about five years old, and after five or six years of lessons had started playing so well that I became curious about the reasons for her progress. I had always enjoyed listening to her practice, and was a typical excited and proud parent when she played in student recitals. On one occasion, though, I became aware for the first time that there was something remarkably *physical* about what she was doing at the keyboard. Put simply, it occurred to me to ask how she could possibly make her fingers go so fast.

Of course, anyone might ask this same question. But to a neurologist (a doctor who takes a special interest in the workings of the brain and muscular system) the question had special significance. My work requires me to know *something* about the function of the brain, and when I realized that I really didn't have the answer to this question, I felt obliged to investigate. My life hasn't been the same since; my own curiosity had blown me a light but fatally seductive kiss, luring me into an affair with a sublime and elusive mystery.

The innocent question "How does she make her fingers go so fast?" had opened a small door to a genuine wonderland. At first, like Lewis Carroll's Alice, I peered through the door as a curious but hopelessly excluded outsider. I undertook a scientifically oriented survey—reading articles and books, attending meetings, and talking to researchers, musicians, and music educators. Then, quite unexpectedly, I fell through to the other side. This happened when I started taking piano lessons.

Let's look at these developments in greater detail. The question, its narrow focus gone, was really this: How do we improve our own physical skills? Guitarists, painters, gymnasts, dancers, jugglers, typists, archers, sushi chefs—the list is long—are creatures with a virtually open-ended capacity to specialize and refine movement. Most of the time we take this ability in ourselves for granted. We have a knack for watch repair or fixing cars (we call it tinkering) and never give it a second thought.

Our interest is not so detached when these skills involve the display of movement for its own sake, or take place in a competitive setting. We cannot resist the urge to see what the body can do when it must perform at the limits of its capabilities. Our appetites as spectators are boundless—we are movement junkies. We spend enormous amounts of money to watch our idols exhibit their prowess at tennis matches, the ballet, in skiing and diving meets, and at demolition derbies. We are unable to resist these demonstrations because they give us a taste of our own fire. It is *we* who are on the stage, or hurtling into the end zone.

Usually we savor the excitement vicariously. It's a lot easier and a lot safer. Some, however, decide to leave the companionship of other spectators to try the experience firsthand. As I learned more about music from the distant comfort of my chair in the library, it became obvious I was missing something critical to an understanding of the musician; as great as his love of music was, his deepest feelings were involved in the act of *making* music. And why shouldn't this be so? The downhill skier, the big-wave surfer, and the gymnast all experience (and cultivate) the feeling of going over the top. It shouldn't matter whether it's the top of a five-octave run or a twenty-foot wave; in the part of the brain that registers excitement and fun, I doubt it makes any difference. Since I could never hope to savor that element of the musical experience unless I tried to learn how to play an instrument, at the age of forty I decided to give it a try.

I now realize that I embarked on this venture with a psychological advantage most adult beginners lack; I knew enough about the way things are hooked up to know that I couldn't miss. It wasn't a question of having access to secret or special knowledge that would make it easier or faster; it was simply a matter of understanding enough about the elegance of human engineering to know that study and practice would produce results. With that knowledge, watching myself as a student became a delightful sideshow. What a kick to be an old dog learning new tricks!

I see absolutely no reason why the same thing shouldn't happen to you. If you are like most people, you would *like* to play an instrument (or sing) but have accepted the myth that musicians have freakish powers and you were left out. Nothing could be further from the truth! Most adults—late bloomers and nonprodigies—are far too modest in their expectations when they try to learn a new skill, and this attitude seems an especially potent deterrent to the recreational enjoyment of music. Somehow we accept the elitist idea that musical competence is limited to the people who were being scouted by Juilliard in the third grade or thereabouts. Too bad; what I didn't know when I started, and urge you to discover for yourself, is that you get a lot better than you really thought you would. In music, as with most things we try to do, failure is rarely caused by poor aptitude; the real culprit is a stunted imagination.

Of course, it is equally self-defeating to begin with the idea that you are on your way to stardom; if the venture is fueled only by a Carnegie Hall fantasy, it won't last three weeks. The high-octane approach is a mistake in music. A thoughtful, ambling pace seems to work best. Happily, you need not worry that your knees will give out before you've made any headway; time is your friend.

Obviously, comparisons between musicians and athletes on the sports field can be overdrawn, but the use of the physical metaphor has both implications and consequences which are far from trivial, or merely poetic. For example, it becomes possible to look specifically at a variety of musical skills, instead of assuming that musicians are simply "musical." There are important similarities, but also great differences, in the musical demands made of a jazz saxophonist and an operatic vocalist. How could they possibly have the same skills, or need the same training program?

Second, the athletic metaphor provides at least the possibility of an objective framework for looking at the roots of success and failure alike. It is too easy to attribute success in music study to innate and rare capacity: "Well, what did you expect? He's not musical at all."

This much is clear: Whatever the truth may be on the matter of talent, it is not enough merely to buy a baseball glove, or a ukulele, in order to become proficient in its use. One also needs a plan, and the time, resolve, and opportunity to put the plan into action. Otherwise the new equipment will just become more clutter in the closet. It seems to me that looking at the physical side of music-making gives us a rational basis for considering the elements of musicianship, and for providing a novel perspective on the training of musicians. In the concluding chapter of the book, we will look at this issue in some detail.

Finally, an understanding of the physical side of music-making, as I suggested in the introduction, can only add to the pleasure of listening for the passionately committed sideliner. Robert Freeman, who is director of the Eastman School of Music at the University of Rochester, New York, often tells audiences about his feelings of bafflement watching a cricket match. "It helps," he says, "to know how the game goes, and the same is true with music." He gives the example of a baseball fan taking pleasure watching the setting up and execution of a double play in baseball, and goes on to say, "If you can't recognize a double play in a Brahms piano concerto, you've missed all the fun." Thus, one's appreciation of a conductor's or an oboist's skill should be enhanced by an understanding not only of the architecture of the music but also of the specific physical challenges its realization requires.

Suppose for now that you hanker to be not on the sidelines but in the middle of the music-makers. It makes sense to ask what you can expect of yourself.

As a general rule, any physical skill exists in us as a potential, and our development of that skill will depend on the specifics of our learning experience (when we started to learn, how we were taught, by whom, and what we ourselves did to apply this instruction). Some people seem to learn faster than others, and in any group of people of similar age and experience, you will find considerable variation in the speed with which most skills are mastered. The quality of peformance (if it can be measured) will fall within a certain range, with most people clustered somewhere near the middle. In other words, a few people lag behind, a few people excel, and most people are close to average. For some strange reason, the people who excel are usually the ones who work the hardest.

In music, far more than in sports, we are intimidated by the enormous difference between our own abilities and those of the pros. There is such a wealth of musical talent around us, and the quality of live and recorded musical performances is so high, that the notion of our competing with the big guys is laughable.

Who said anything about competing? Does our apparent unsuitability for a money-making musical career mean we have no right to buy a guitar or a harmonica and carry on with our friends, or bring an instrument with us on a weekend camping trip?

The question of age is often a concern to those planning to

begin. I have been asked on any number of occasions, "When is it too late to begin?" The answer, if your interest is recreational, is plainly that it is never too late.

A friend of mine recently introduced me to a woman in her nineties. Ellen, I will call her, is a widow who hasn't time to sit still. Several years ago, at age eighty-eight, she went to a music store in San Francisco and inquired about the purchase of an organ. The salesman, either by word or by gesture, gave her the strong impression that he did not take her interest seriously, so she left. Two stores later, still asking the same questions, she got a different look from the salesman. This time she was asked about previous musical experience. "I think I may have had some singing in school in the fourth or fifth grade, but I don't remember much about it," she answered.

Either it was a slow month or the salesman was truly evangelistic about his work, because he smiled at this reply and said: "It'll come back!"

Ellen told me this story over lunch, and with considerable glee insisted that the music from her singing classes *had* come back. Now, some five years later, she has "traded up" organs seven times, plays in her home at all hours (she can listen to herself through headphones), and declares: "I've got more burned pots in my kitchen than anybody I know in this county."

Another encounter with a late bloomer is worth repeating here, because it makes a somewhat different point about music and its appeal when the goal is personal satisfaction. I had been invited to talk about music on a radio program in Chicago and the question of age had come up. A woman caller identified herself as the sixty-year-old wife of a professional trumpet player. "I was never able to join in his activities," she said. "I was left out. About six months ago I decided to take drum lessons, and I can't tell you how much fun I'm having. I think I'm getting good, but that doesn't matter. What I think people should know is that I found there were things I could say with the drums I've never been able to say before. I can't even tell you what I mean, but it's true." It was obvious from her voice that practice for her was not drudgery—apparently it was now what she lived for.

One is obliged to ask whether these anecdotes are genuinely instructive on the question of age and musical ability; is there really any prospect that older people can begin the study of music and expect to get anywhere with it? As it turns out, there is a substantial record of important research on the subject of brain changes (and mental competence) related to age, and this work suggests that we may greatly underestimate both the capacity for learning and the value of active study in later life.[1]

Dr. Marian Diamond, a highly regarded neuroanatomist at the University of California at Berkeley, has had considerable fun recently telling people about her work with elderly rats. Both in behavioral tests and in careful anatomic studies of the brains of these animals, she and her colleagues have demonstrated repeatedly that senility has more to do with environment and inactivity than with age. If older rats are kept in an enriched environment and fed a steady diet of interesting challenges, they'll outsmart younger and faster competitors every time. As Marian says of the brain, "Keep using it or lose it; it's as simple as that old cliché."[2]

At the other end of the age scale we have a profoundly different question, namely, when is it too early to begin? Since our focus is on adults, I prefer to make only passing comment about young children in music. I have spoken with many experienced and thoughtful teachers who work with small children in music instruction, and there seems to be wide agreement that when children are given the chance to explore, and are taught on the basis of what they can be expected to discern, understand, and accomplish for their age, they learn very rapidly and are learning more than imitation.

They take readily to situations where they are encouraged to improvise (even to compose) and to play in ensembles. Their ability to discriminate pitch is extremely good, and it is apparently not difficult for them to acquire highly accurate pitch discrimination before the age of five. Young children's interest in music is strongly influenced by parental involvement and support. And, as I have already indicated, the reverse is equally true!

I think the musician-athlete thesis can be briefly summarized: Questions of aesthetics aside, music-making is at its foundation a physical act, involving the refinement of bodily movement for the creation and shaping of meaningful sound. From the moment you begin, the way you hear and the way you touch will be changed. You will develop a personal relationship with a strange-looking object that will become an extension of you.*

Regardless of the age at which you begin, or the instrument you choose, you will encounter a set of conditions which form a stable working context, or neighborhood: There are ideas and materials to be explored, teachers to guide you, tools to be mastered, and a personal discipline you must establish and refine as you go along. It would be the same if you were taking up archery—in one case *arrows* fly off the bow, in the other it's *music.*

The way the musician's brain sees the problem (we'll ignore for now the complexities of controlling a specific instrument), learning to play a piece begins with learning the notes that are in it. There are several ways to do this. The notes may be printed on a page in a code which you read and convert into movements; you may hear the notes and remember them well enough to reproduce them; you may hear them inside your head and du-

*People become attached to their instruments, sometimes in amusing and sometimes in poignant ways. Clarinet and brass players will swear that they can play with only one mouthpiece, and, emulating kids with magical baseball mitts or hockey sticks, may sleep with their secret weapon. As with bowling balls, though, most musical instruments make poor bedfellows.

plicate them on an instrument (composers and musicians who improvise are very good at this). Or the notes may be given in a *spoken* code ("Play me a C sharp, George," the singer may say softly to her piano player before she begins her song, and George finds the key on the piano, in her voice range, that strikes a string tuned to play a C sharp).

Whatever method is used, you will adopt the intended sequence of notes as a plan for carrying out the movements that will yield, on the instrument being played, the correct sequence of sounds. How will you know if you have got it right?

Think of a tune or a song you know well enough to hear the note sequence, with approximately correct pitch, in your head. Can't think of one? Try "Happy Birthday." If you have an instrument whose pitch you can control (including your own voice), you should be able to play the same melody after a little experimenting, even though you don't know the names of the notes or their precise musical relationships. Suppose now that you are asked to play a melody you are not familiar with. How would you know you had played it correctly?

As it happens, you are the proud owner of four different physiologic mechanisms which enable you to detect and remember the results of your musical efforts. (You also possess detection systems, such as your sense of smell, which don't help a great deal with music.) These systems are the foundation of what are referred to as perceptual skills, and can be used alone or together anytime you are playing an instrument. They are as follows:

1. Visual—you can watch to see that your fingers hit the correct notes;
2. Auditory—you can listen as you play to make sure that the notes follow the pattern you expect to hear;
3. Tactile—you can detect the mechanical contact your fingers, lips, and tongue make with your instrument,

and make accurate judgments about pressure, temperature, and texture of the surface being touched;

4. Kinesthetic—you can feel changes in muscle and joint position as you manipulate the instrument, and use this information to adjust the muscular contractions used to control the instrument (much of this information is unconscious).

In addition to these so-called primary sensory modalities, you have available to you a uniquely human system that helps you to synthesize and correlate information in useful ways and that allows you to monitor your performance through external observations. This information may come to you after what is, in physiologic terms, enormous delay, and yet may have extraordinary impact on your development. For simplicity, I will refer to this system as:

5. Verbal—a knowledgeable observer who watches and listens can report to you what you did; this is what a teacher does, and what the critics insist on doing (whether you want them to or not!). In addition, you are always free to talk to yourself.

In purely physical terms, it matters very little which of these monitoring systems you use to improve your playing, regardless of the method you happen to rely on to translate notes into music. As you will discover in the chapter on sight reading, there are times when you will want to deny yourself access to information available to you. In most cases we use a perceptual blend to judge our success and plan corrective action when the results do not satisfy us. For obvious reasons, our sense of hearing (auditory perception) will become enshrined as the final arbiter.

However *physical* music-making may be, it is more than that. It is, in a very special way, a bridge to what I suppose must be called the creative impulse. Let me explain. Like all moving creatures, humans have a central nervous system that regulates the body in its interactions with the outside world. Because we are primates—mammals who walk upright—our upper limbs are not needed to support our body weight against gravity. With this mechanical arrangement of our posture in relation to gravity, there has always existed for mankind the opportunity to use hands and arms for an endless variety of specialized tasks. Coexisting with that opportunity we find an enormous elaboration in the brain of a motor control system which seems dedicated to the extraordinary refinement of movement of our upper limbs.

We also have the gift of exceptional control of the muscles of the face and oral cavity, and brain mechanisms for controlling these muscles just as precisely as we control those of our upper limbs. Human language and song have been the result.

Other animals can fly on their own power, climb faster and higher, jump farther, and swim deeper than we do. No other animals paint, write sonnets or editorials, sing barber shop quartets, or play the fiddle.

If you consider any human activity which has ever been called creative, you will find an example of carefully planned, highly skilled movements guided by the body's small muscles in service of another peculiarly human trait—the instinct for communication. Music, because it is such an effective and immediate communicator of feelings, has developed into a powerful voice not only for the individual but for society. Its capacity to communicate simultaneously what is personal and what is universal endows it with the cultural importance it is accorded in most societies. Because of the highly developed notation used for documenting (and, in the twentieth century, for recording) performance, music also stands as one of the most significant forms of expression by which any civilization can inform history of its cultural life.

Ansel Adams, the venerated American photographer, spoke about his own creativity using a musical metaphor. He said that "viewing the photographic negative was like viewing a composer's score, since each displays a static set of symbols which intend a statement of personal feeling or vision. Their ultimate purpose is to be brought to life by an interpreter (photographer or musical performer) who, in the process of printing or performance, inevitably includes his or her own personal imagery of sound or vision."[3]

Is it so fanciful to compare a musical score to a photographic negative, and to compare the photographer who develops the print to a conductor leading an orchestra? I think not. Nor is it a surprise that Adams might ask us to understand his work in this way.

Creativity is inextricably bound up with change and movement. A creative act must involve the communication of a point of view, which is made possible because someone moves, sees, compares, reflects, and then decides to let others know about the experience. As a young man, Adams had trained for a career as a concert pianist. He gave up the idea because he felt he could not develop the required technique, but for the rest of his life continued to play for his own enjoyment. One of his students and a close personal friend was Rosario Mazzeo, for many years the bass clarinetist for the Boston Symphony Orchestra as well as chairman of the woodwind department of the New England Conservatory of Music. Mazzeo made many recordings of Adams at the piano (after he had "given it up") and often plays them for visitors. He says the most critical and attentive listeners are musicians. Because of Adams' beautiful tone and eloquent phrasing, they usually feel they are hearing one of the great pianists—

possibly one of the immortals. He had a great deal to say, more than one way to express himself, and certainly *was* one of the immortals in photography.

Notes

1. Roger Walsh, *Towards an Ecology of Brain,* Spectrum Publications, 1981. (P. 164 contains a bibliography of scientific papers by Dr. Diamond and colleagues on this topic.)
2. Quoted in Erica Goode, "Some Good News About Growing Old," *San Francisco Chronicle,* May 10, 1983.
3. Rosario Mazzeo, personal letter to author, August 16, 1985.

2

Pumping Ivory

AN INTRODUCTION TO THE SMALL-MUSCLE ATHLETE

When you were young, probably less than five years old, you learned how to tie your shoelaces. This is a big moment in a kid's life, and I have no trouble at all recalling how excited I was at this triumph in my own case. I am reasonably certain I had been struggling for months over the difficulties, until one day during a midafternoon naptime, I realized I had broken the code. I tied the shoes once, tied them again to be sure, then tumbled out of the crib to show my mother what I had done. I knew at that moment not only that I had learned something very important but that I had proven I was too old to be confined to a crib after lunch.

Nearly forty years later this exalted feeling swept over me again when, for the first time in my life, I put together the first few measures of the canon in a Bach Invention. In case you are unfamiliar with canons and Bach Inventions, it is easier to explain than to execute them. In a canon, a melody begins in one voice (or hand on the keyboard), and very soon another voice or the other hand joins in with the same melody (as in "Row, Row, Row Your Boat"). What happens next is limited only by the ingenuity of the composer, and J. S. Bach was very ingenious. His Inventions are shorter keyboard works written to teach young students how to listen to, and play, two or more melodic lines at once. In a sense, the interweaving musical ideas are tied together just as the shoelaces are.

Perhaps it is farfetched to compare canons and shoelaces; it is *not* difficult to see the similarities in the physical movements that produce them. In your mind's eye, take away the piano, and the laces, and what do you see? You see two hands moving apart and together again, with the fingers moving independently and mimicking or echoing each other's movements in what is almost a miniature dance. The individual movements are smooth, gentle, and efficient. They seem casual, but in fact are a precisely controlled sequence of muscle and joint movements rehearsed to such a level of consistency that the result of their cooperative efforts is virtually always the same.

In reality, much of our ordinary physical activity is made up of movements like these, which have become so automatic that we hardly notice what we are doing as we carry them out. We comb our hair, sign our name, dial the telephone, button our buttons, drive a car, swing a tennis racket or a golf club, entirely oblivious of the system which controls the movements we use to carry out these tasks.

Eventually, tying one's shoelaces becomes a completely mindless activity, giving rise to no particular sense of accomplishment. One's conscious involvement in the playing of a canon (or any other piece of music) does not fade so quickly. The musician does not lose interest in a piece of music once the notes have been learned. On the contrary, learning a sequence of moves to produce sounds coming from an instrument is only the first step. After this comes the task of making the sounds into music.

If you were never going to undertake anything more complex than combing your hair, it would not make any difference whether you understood how you are able to manage your own grooming. However, it makes a great deal of sense to know something about what's under your own hood if you intend to explore the limits of your own physical capabilities, or want to understand why some efforts succeed and others do not.

Otto Ortmann published his landmark monograph *The Phys-*

iological Mechanics of Piano Technique in 1929, and in the bibliography cited no fewer than seventy-three references under the heading of "Physiology of Piano Technique," of which eight were published before 1890. Yet, as Ortmann says in the Preface to his volume, these books, "when they are found in the teacher's library at all, too often still have their leaves uncut."[1]

There must be any number of explanations for the failure of such futuristic thinking to stir revolutionary fires in music education; I can think of at least two, and will reflect on these (and their impact) in the book's concluding chapter on music study.

Meanwhile, it is interesting to contemplate the effect of similarly novel (but reversely oriented) thinking on the fortunes of one of the large-muscle disciplines, that of the bodybuilders. If ever there were a subculture with an image problem, and insecurity galore, this was it. The undisputed laughingstock of middle class beer drinkers for generations, they turned it all around overnight by making their exertions faintly thoughtful and scientific, and putting on a high tech, high fashion look. If you don't know what I'm talking about, take a look at their journals and equipment catalogs. They gave up trying to be different and joined forces with a lot of other happy people. Not so dumb after all. It is possible, furthermore, that attitudes and practices associated with fitness training have actually been changed, and are more appealing because they somehow make more sense to the nonfanatic.

If the bodybuilders have finessed their image problem, and enlivened their discipline so handily, musicians might have something to gain by a frontal assault on the entrenched view within and outside the profession that they are disembodied priests of a secular religion. In other words, the musicians might consider opening their own eyes, and those of the rest of the world, to the notion that what they are engaged in is essentially *physical* in nature.

In the previous chapter, an attempt was made to confront seriously the idea of the musician as an athlete—that the pianist might be regarded as a cousin to the heavily muscled weightlifter "pumping iron," except that he is using small muscles and pumping *ivory*.

Of course, nothing seems more contrary than the notion that musical skills might be muscular in the same sense that traditional sports skills are muscular. Deep within our collective memory is the imprint of the bespectacled, frail, and passive kid instantly recognized as being musical. Having been impressed at an early age with the heroic mythology of the locker room, the word *muscle* evokes for us images of mass, strength, and combat. We all know about biceps, triceps, deltoids, and "pecs," but whoever heard of somebody having a knockout set of abductor digiti quinti minimi, or a breathtaking flexor pollicis brevis? As noted above, musicians themselves have sometimes fallen prey to the notion that bulk is what counts in the muscle department. It is a colorful notion, and false.

Musical skill depends upon movements in which the entire body participates, but is built on precise control of the smaller muscles of the arms and hands, or those of the vocal and respiratory tracts, or both. The musician, a small-muscle athlete, is not just a big athlete in miniature. No other activity in which we engage requires the accuracy, speed, timing, smoothness, or coordination of muscular contraction exhibited in finished musical performance.

Muscles (even the bulky ones) are more than a set of coiled springs, or the ultimate male adornment in Southern California. They are an extension of the brain (just as the ears and eyes are), the action end of an integrated neurophysiologic system designed for interaction of the body with its surroundings. When the interaction is between the musician and an instrument, the muscular system becomes a synthesizer of combined output for a host of neurologic subsystems involved in hearing, vision, movement, language, and emotion. When one examines the anatomy and physiology of the motor system, one sees in the logic of its organization a message about priorities: It is a system in which flexible control and variable responsiveness of the small muscles represent the pinnacle of development.

I have gone to some lengths to argue that the musician and his counterpart on the athletic field are not so different in their skills, or in the difficulties and rewards they experience as they develop and try their talents. When you ignore the size of the muscles called into play, many of the differences seem to fade into insignificance. But I have also suggested that there *are* important differences—that the small-muscle athlete is not just a miniature football player. It is now appropriate to look more closely at the details.

If you have ever watched an orchestra closely, you will probably have noticed that when the violinists play in unison they make not only the same sounds but almost exactly the same movements. At times they begin to look like a ballet corps (perhaps this is one of the reasons audiences continue to enjoy live performance of symphonic music, despite the excellence of recordings). This synchronization of movements by the entire ensemble is not planned for visual effect; it occurs because there tends to be close agreement among advanced musicians about the preferred way to play a given passage on any instrument.

Clearly, the musical instrument itself has considerable bearing on the physical processes of music-making. Since different instruments generate sound in different ways, the particular movements used to play a score will of course depend on the instrument being used. A flute player, a violinist, and a pianist may each play the same melody, and even play it together as a trio playing in unison, but in so doing each will tailor the movements to the instrument as well as to the piece being played. The design of the instrument has important consequences for everyone involved in the musical experience: composer, musician, and listener.

Although our primary concern here relates to the physical aspects of playing a particular instrument, it is not easy to distinguish these from what seem to be aesthetic considerations. The composer often chooses an instrument or a combination of instruments because of a desire to match the sound, or voice, of the music to its message. There may also be a special concern about voice mixtures—what instruments create a desired effect in ensemble. The musician tends to select for his personal use an instrument whose sound is valued—this means not only choosing a saxophone over a flute, for example, but finding the saxophone that has just the right sound texture, or timbre (we will go into this in greater detail in the section on auditory perception in music). And the listener may go to hear a horn concerto because of a special affection for the sound of the French horn, or to a guitar, piano, or flute recital for similar reasons.

At the same time, instrument choice (for composer, musician, or listener) may turn on what seems to be a straightforward manipulative or visual trait: For the composer, the question might be how fast the instrument can play a passage that has to be blazingly rapid; for the musician, how heavy is the instrument, or how well suited to the size and shape of lips or fingers; for the listener, how well can he see what the musician is doing?

Let us consider the seemingly trivial difference between the harpsichord and the piano. The harpsichord, the most important keyboard instrument in use at the time of Bach, is operated by depressing a key which causes a string, or paired strings, to be plucked. Its major limitation is that there is no way for the player to vary the loudness of its sound—that is, to control its dynamics—solely by finger pressure. In the early eighteenth century, probably in 1709, a Paduan harpsichord builder named

Bartolomeo Cristofori invented a mechanism which permitted the strings to be struck, rather than plucked, so that the instrument could be played soft or loud according to touch. That distinction is the basis of the formal name of this instrument—pianoforte—which means, literally, soft-loud. Because of this simple engineering change (with far-reaching acoustic consequences), the hand was given a job it had not had to manage at the keyboard before.

The rapid evolution of the piano as a concert instrument certainly has a great deal to do with its acoustic power and with its capacity to satisfy the need for volume in performances in large halls or with sizable ensembles. But it is possible that the piano was destined to eclipse the harpsichord anyway, because it presented the skilled musician with a new and different set of control problems, associated with its greatly expanded dynamic range.

So the musician, along with the tennis player and the archer, is confronted with what in scientific or engineering parlance is known as a "control" problem. He or she must adapt the use of some part of the body to an external object in order to make the object behave in a particular and predictable way.

Football players, soccer players, and baseball players spend a great deal of time, as do musicians, doing drills and learning patterns of movement involving manipulation of an object of some kind. With the obvious exception of divers and gymnasts, competitive athletes virtually never play the same game twice, and therefore need not anticipate and rehearse every move that will be performed, in sequence, before a contest. Unless he is improvising, the musician must do exactly this if an acceptable level of public performance is to be achieved. Even when the music is improvisational, much of the performance may consist of last-minute assemblies of standard routines rehearsed many times previously. Most often, though, the mu[illegible] the notes given in a score, like the stage actor [illegible] lines are fixed by the script. In that case, he remai[illegible] strict obligation to play what the composer has writte[illegible] matter how he brings his music to life, the experienced musicia[illegible] will build his performance on a foundation of finely choreographed, precisely ordered small-muscle movements. Reliable control of the instrument and smooth execution of the score could not occur otherwise.

However wondrous the rehearsed performance of a lengthy score may be (and it is wondrous!), it is not enough to warrant the claim that the musician is doing something more complex than his counterpart on the athletic field. What sets the musician apart is the ability, superimposed on what has already been described, to adjust and refine the smallest details of movement as necessary to fine-tune, adjust, and coax out of the instrument sounds that come alive. This may require something so ordinary as adjusting the pitch of a vibrating string so that it stays within a range of 440 to 442 cycles per second while it is being bowed, or something so complex as creating the illusion that the voice of a French horn is that of an impish, playful boy, projected above the other voices of a full symphonic orchestra. The achievement of this illusion requires something more than manual and lingual dexterity, though it cannot occur in the absence of such skill.

Whatever the specific choice of instrument or favorite style of music, in the final analysis the musician's primary task is to exploit whatever sound-making potential exists in his collaboration with composer, the composer's music, his own instrument, and those within earshot who are interested in the proceedings. This is the goal for performance of any given piece of music, and it is the overriding career goal of the musician. This means number of things. At the most fundamental level, it means learning the moves required just to play the notes accurately. At the most advanced level, it means developing an ear for the range of moods that can be suggested by variations in style and technique of play, and the ability to bring any desired sound out of the instrument, whenever it is called for in the music, rain or shine. Somewhere in the middle the task is to develop his own ideas of musical expression, and his own taste, and to learn how to call on his technical skills to bring his interpretive ideas about the music into being. That's what the study of music is for, and why it never ceases.

Now let's look at the specialists in this job: the body's small muscles. Let's assume for the moment that when you approach a musical instrument for the first time you have had some experience either with a typewriter, adding machine, or computer terminal. Speed in any of these activities depends on regulating the separate and skillful movements of individual fingers, which are called fractionation movements. Similar kinds of finger movement are required for playing almost every musical instrument. Some instruments require more than this: The organ demands skilled movement of the feet as well as the hands and arms; wind instruments demand control of the facial and intraoral muscles to produce a pleasing tone. Wind instrumentalists (and vocalists) must also develop exceptional control of the air stream used to set up vibrations in the oscillator on which their sound is built. This is true, no matter what one might think, even for the sweet music of the bagpipe. String players have the interesting problem of controlling pitch with one hand and arm (normally the left, which is fascinating in itself), dynamics and timbre with the other, and the timing and sequencing of tones by collaboration of the pair.

How do they do it? In the most general terms, it is correct to say that the process by which a musician achieves a musical goal during performance requires the painstaking composition of a neuromuscular score to guide the physical movements on which the performance is built. This is true because in order for our movements to be effective, the brain (and particularly the motor system) must regulate the degree of contraction and relaxation of every muscle participating in a particular move, at every instant, or exact control could not occur. The physiologic score, by the way, can be one which prescribes economy and precision of movement, or a laborious and inefficient execution of the movements demanded for realization of the composer's intent. The muscles, within their physical limitations, will do what they are told.

May we have a concrete example, maestro? We will take a simple case, not requiring the fine-tuning of pitch by the hand. Suppose we have decided to tackle "Mary Had a Little Lamb" on the keyboard. There are three different white keys in each octave on which we can start this piece and play it through without having to leave the white keys. We have ten digits to choose from with which to depress the keys, and we can use any combination we choose. We can play the piece with the same finger of one or both hands (the hunt and peck system) or we can try to assign particular fingers to particular keys according to a plan. When we do this, we are working out the fingering for our piece. Keyboard artists usually look for fingerings which make movement comfortable, and leave their hands in position to cover the keys that need to be played without getting themselves into a corner. We don't need to get into the art and science of fingering here; the point is that there is usually good reason to think these assignments through if you have time.

Call your five fingers by letter name: thumb, index, middle, ring, small (T, I, M, R, S) and imagine yourself working out the fingering of "Mary Had a Little Lamb" (you really don't need the piano to do this—a tabletop works fine if you don't mind using your imagination). For me, playing this song is easiest with the sequence M I T I M M M, I I I, M S S (and so on). This might not work particularly well for you if the thumb of the right hand tends to miss the note assigned to it, or feels clumsy compared to the other fingers being used.

Without pondering the problem at great length, most people would simply elect to shift one finger over, adding the ring finger and deleting the thumb, to see how that works. This trial revision of strategy occurs to us without a great deal of thought or conscious analysis, because of our previous experience using our hands. A more radical (and somehow unnatural) alternative would be to decide that the hand was inappropriate for this job, and to try to employ the nose to get the job done. There is, incidentally, nothing inherently wrong with playing the piano with one's nose; it's just that experience (or our teacher) tells us there are any number of more effective ways to play.

Now suppose that you are a fledgling pianist. You have located the keys on the piano which produce the notes of the entire melody you wish to play. By a process of trial and error you have established the sequence in which the keys must be depressed to duplicate the melody. At this stage, you are using what physiologists refer to as a system of *current control* to guide your efforts. This means that you plan the move in some way ("Hit that key over there"), initiate the move ("Here goes!"), and listen for the result ("Hey, that was it!"). These comments to yourself serve here as markers for the stages normally involved in conscious planning of a simple movement, setting it in motion, and following its progress and outcome.

Having succeeded at this, you return proudly to your teacher, who listens, smiles, and then says to you: "That was excellent. Now, see if you can make it *sing!*"

Notes

1. Otto Ortmann, *The Physiological Mechanics of Piano Technique,* E. P. Dutton, 1929. Reprinted in Da Capo Press Music Reprint Series, 1981.

3

Fast Fingers and Hot Chops

WHY YOU WON'T BE A KLUTZ FOREVER

He flies through the ayre
With the greatest of ease
The pipes sing their song
When the bag gets a squeeze.

But how does he know
When to squeeze, when to puff?
It's all in the head—
Doesn't that say enough?*

It is a good rule of thumb that you can guess how much is known about a subject from the number of books written about it: the more books, the less is known. If you were to add up all the books written about the brain, including those written by psychiatrists, neurologists, psychologists, neurophysiologists, and neurosurgeons, you'd have almost as many books as there are about government. There is, of course, no shortage of books about music.

By no means does this imply that it is a waste of time to read (or, I hope, write) books on a topic with a reputation for keeping researchers, authors, and the publishing industry up after bed-time. It should simply serve as a reminder that most important

*All the good Lewis Carroll quotations suitable for chapter openings have long since been used up. The reason for this bit of doggerel will become clear at the end of the final chapter. Wait until you get there.

areas of human interest and inquiry breed questions faster than answers. You can reasonably expect, therefore, to progress through the thoughtful literature on almost any serious topic with an increasing sense of amazement and mystification. You should also smell a ruse if something you read purports to give you the truth, or a final answer, about anything trickier than the preferred method to get safely through a revolving door.

In this and several of the succeeding chapters, we will examine a variety of fascinating ideas concerning the role of the brain in music-making. However, I assure you that this review is not intended to explain how the brain works or how we make music. I personally don't know how the brain works, doubt that anyone else does, and am not even sure I want to know. Moreover, and emphatically, I declare that this is *not* a book intended to explore, reiterate, amplify, or (forgive me!) regurgitate what has already appeared regarding the right side of the brain.*

In the previous chapter, it was said that "the process by which a musician achieves a musical goal during performance requires the composition of a *neurophysiologic* score to guide the physical movements on which the performance is built." What does this metaphor mean? It means that movement takes place because of muscular contraction, that muscular contraction is regulated by the nervous system, and that skilled movement is a process that requires advance planning for optimal results. This whole process is controlled by the brain—*both* sides of it.

*I share the widespread fascination, explored abundantly in published essays, with clinical studies revealing that the left and right sides of the brain employ different strategies in processing information. I don't know how these findings apply to learning in people with their original anatomy intact, and wish the Right Brain Bandwagon were more patient and less noisy. The compulsive tendency of official protectors of the right brain to spread their exhortations in print recalls a professor's acrid comments about research reports in his own field: "I am reminded of the locomotion of a squid," he said, "an animal that moves backward emitting great quantities of ink."

Our examination of this physiologic composition will proceed in the following steps. First, we will touch on muscle activity, and the anatomic and physiologic arrangements which guide the collaboration of groups of muscles. Second, we will look at some broad concepts of neurologic regulation of motor activity. Third, we will look at the functional organization of the motor control system of the brain, and examine the differences between control of simple, unplanned movement and that involved in highly skilled movement. We will then consider what might be involved in preserving flexible control of highly automatized movement.

Large or small, all muscle is specialized tissue in the body whose function is to change its length. The muscles used to move bones and joints are called skeletal muscles (to distinguish them from muscles of our inner organs), and it is these we are interested in.

Because of the attachment of nerves to its surface, a skeletal muscle is capable of responding to volleys of electrical signals originating in the spinal cord (which, in turn, usually takes its marching orders from the brain). The muscles whose names we are familiar with (biceps, hamstrings, and so forth) are made up of countless individual muscle fibers called motor units. These can contract singly, or together with other muscle fibers that make up the entire muscle. The capacity of motor units to act independently or in concert accounts for the extraordinary range of force and speed seen in the contractility of skeletal muscle.

A muscle contracts only when it is instructed to; in the absence of nerve stimulation, muscle is inert. The control signals, or impulses, carried by the nerve cause a chemical reaction to occur within the substance of the muscle, whereby a stored form of energy is released, causing the muscle fibers to become shorter. A few impulses produce a twitch, and repeated stimulation causes increasingly forceful contraction. The arrangement is such that smaller fibers begin to contract first, with slight force. As stimulation increases, more and more fibers join the contraction with greater and greater force.

Almost as soon as the muscle begins to contract, it initiates another reaction to reverse the effect of the nerve stimulation. Consequently, extremely precise and rapid adjustment of contraction and relaxation is possible.

We need to bear in mind that muscles can provide both propelling and braking force. Sometimes braking is necessary to stop or reverse the movement of a limb (as in bowing a stringed instrument). The effect can also occur in more passive ways. Muscle is not gossamer; it has weight, viscosity, and tensile strength and can therefore influence (usually resist) bodily movement even when not an active participant. For this reason, athletes who are concerned about speed often limit training that tends to increase muscle bulk, fearing they may become "muscle bound."

There are two other ways by which muscle can slow (actually get in the way of) movement. First, a mechanism exists in the spinal cord to initiate active contraction of a muscle when it is being stretched. You pull on the muscle and it will pull back. This is an automatic reflex thought to have a number of useful functions (it keeps you from landing on your nose when you are walking, running, or going downstairs, and it seems to decrease the risk that a muscle could be injured by overstretching).*

It is worth knowing about this unconscious mechanism, because it can be amplified by a variety of influences capable of modifying the physiology of the nervous system, including anxiety and caffeine. Heightened responsiveness of muscle often creates chronic neck and back pain in people under psychological

*When your doctor taps on your knee with his reflex hammer, your leg jumps because the upper thigh muscle has been instantaneously stretched and is responding dutifully.

pressure, and can degrade the smoothness of muscle activity in any skilled performance.

The second mechanism responsible for involuntary active muscle contraction is of great theoretical interest and importance to musicians. In a sense, it is a shadow or default mechanism, because it emerges as a consequence of the failure, or reduced effectiveness, of an active system to *relax* muscle.

It might not be apparent that there should ever be a need to *force* muscles to relax. That is, if muscles contract when the switch is turned on, don't they relax when it is turned off? The answer is, yes, they do—but the relaxation may not come soon enough or it may be incomplete. Let's step into the biomechanics lab for just a moment.

The necessity to induce muscular relaxation actively occurs for two principal reasons: first, because muscle teamwork is what produces bodily movement; second, because a muscle or muscle group may be doing more than one job at once, and may finish one job before finishing another.

In most cases there are many muscles arranged around the body's moving joints, and they position the underlying bones wherever needed by a process of balanced contraction and relaxation. It is easy to see this on yourself.

If you will inspect your own upper arm, holding your palm up, you can feel the biceps muscle on top taking the load. The triceps muscle, suspended underneath when the arm is held like this, should be loose and flabby. Now, if you will gradually straighten out the arm and lay the back of your hand on a flat surface (desk or table would be best) and start to push down, you will feel the biceps relax and the triceps tighten up. This is a simple and valuable demonstration of what is called agonist and antagonist action of muscles. When one pulls, its partner relaxes so as to make the job easier.

Now move your hand down just past the elbow of the arm

you are feeling. Wiggle the fingers of one arm while feeling the forearm muscles with the hand of the other arm. Drum your fingers as fast as you can on a tabletop, and watch and feel what happens in the same forearm muscles.

The point of this part of the demonstration is straightforward: Bodily movement always occurs because of a combination of muscular contractions and relaxations working in cooperation. It is easy to detect the interchange by simple inspection of your own arm. Intuition should lead you to suspect that very fast reversals of direction (as in finger drumming) would require *abrupt* relaxation of opposing muscles for maximum efficiency. Without some method for inhibition, the violinist, guitarist, or pianist would be confined to playing serenades and lullabies. The existence of this mechanism has been amply confirmed in the laboratory, many times over.

What about incomplete relaxation? Try this: Hold one arm over your head, and place the opposite hand on the shoulder muscle (deltoid, if you want to be technical), feeling for the firmness of contraction. Now let the arm fall to your side. Notice the change in firmness of the deltoid as the arm goes through the midportion of the drop, and as it nears the lowest point. If you pay close attention, you will notice that there is a phase of relaxation (the muscle gets soft) and then contraction again (the muscle gets firm). Do you remember trying to stop the fall of the arm? Try it again and do the best you can to keep your deltoid muscle from contracting at the end of the fall. Not so easy, is it?

What you have observed is an involuntary contraction, built into the control system and highly responsive to the effects of gravity on all of your movements. That includes the movements made by the small muscles of the hands and arms. The only way this system can be inactivated is by going after it with a club. It has to be *forced* to turn off.

The implications of these arrangements should give us reverent pause, for several reasons. First, and in the broadest sense, we are led immediately to an appreciation that muscles are not simply *arranged* around bones and joints; they are *organized* functionally and synergistically to permit mechanical versatility and efficiency of skeletal movement (no matter what, or how many things at once, we are doing). Second, it should be clear that the mechanical potential would be wasted without a biologic computer capable of dictating instantaneously the precise details of the full panoply of contractions and relaxations throughout the course of organized movement, sunup to sundown, seven days a week.

The full import of these considerations was recognized and cited over a hundred years ago: The brain is controlling more than muscles—it is controlling movements. In 1873, Dr. Hughlings Jackson, a pioneer theorist in the neurologic control of movement, proposed this conceptualization,[1] and neurophysiologists have been trying to work out the details ever since.[2]

Dr. Jackson may or may not have had musicians in mind; we do, and should be intrigued by the following report:

> Schumann's C major Toccata, Op. 7, has 6266 notes and, as played by Simon Barere without the repeat, requires 4 minutes and 20 seconds—a speed of 24.1 notes per second. . . . For any finger to go into action [flexion and extension movements may occur in any or all of the three finger joints, side-to-side movements may occur, and] at least two fingers must be moved out of the road, involving [other] motor actions. So without counting the motions of the wrist, forearm, shoulder and trunk, or those involving the use of the pedals, a speed of 20 to 30 notes per second may involve 400 to 600 separate motor actions [per second!]—all effected by a competent musician with such automatism that he can give his attention to the overall effects, rather than to the mechanical details.[3]

We are now ready to consider what is known of the answer to the question that got me started on all this: "How does she make her fingers go so fast?" I now recognize that the question, as posed, becomes far more interesting to musicians if appended to read: ". . . and still manage to make it so musical!"

A muscle will contract when stimulated by its nerve, which carries messages from the spinal cord. The principal source of those messages is a cluster of neurons called the anterior horn cells, so named because of the shape they make within the central portion of the spinal cord.

The anterior horn cells, together with smaller cells nearby with which they are in contact, are under the control of higher neuronal centers in the brain, and operate as though they were "smart" relay stations. This is because they monitor each other's activity, gather and interpret sensory information from nerve endings in muscle, skin, and joints, and modify outgoing instruction to muscles under their control so that you're not always stepping on your own toes, as it were. Among other things, this relay system is a facilitator and expediter for the start and stop orders to agonist and antagonist muscles.

Up on top, where the sun shines, the motor system is organized in a way that tempts us to imagine its being composed of three separate but highly integrated subsystems. Recognizing that we are only inventing components for our own convenience, we will nevertheless submit to the temptation.

The first part of the system we will consider is called the motor strip, or motor cortex. It is visible on the surface of the exposed brain, running ear to ear across the top as a narrow band of cortex just in front of a prominent groove called the Rolandic fissure. The motor strip contains the brain's largest neurons (called Betz cells), which make direct contact with the surface of anterior horn cells in the spinal cord.

The Betz cells are connected with groups of neurons immediately in front of the motor strip, as well as with the other two components of the motor system we have yet to discuss. Because of its dominant influence over muscle contraction, and the extensive connections with virtually all of the rest of the brain, this narrow band of brain tissue is uniquely situated to select and orchestrate our motor behavior.

The motor strip could legitimately be called the hub of the motor system. Interestingly, it is one of the areas of the brain where we can construct a topical map of brain activity that roughly suggests the shape of the body. Some years ago, Dr. Wilder Penfield and his colleagues at the Montreal Neurological Institute discovered that a very weak electrical stimulus applied to individual points on the motor strip would cause muscles in various locations of the body to twitch. After doing this repeatedly in a number of patients, they were able to say with a great deal of confidence which parts of the motor strip were responsible for activating which muscles of the body.[4] Their findings led to the development of a facsimile of the human body stretched across the motor strip, which they called the homunculus.

Their homunculus is the map of a body that is all hands, tongue, mouth, and face. Its graphic message is that the bulk of the motor control system is assigned to the smaller muscles of the body, namely the muscles of the hands and arms and those involved in vocalization. You can't spend much time thinking about this arrangement without suspecting humans were cut out to be musicians.

Of course, carrying out any purposeful movement (and this includes playing the kazoo) necessarily involves a good deal more than just twitching the small muscles; as we have already stressed, muscles have to work smoothly in collaboration with one another in complex and constantly changing patterns of contraction and relaxation. Timing and sequence of contraction as well as precise control of force and speed are essential, and involve the active participation of the other components of the system.

The next component of the motor system we will consider is not visible at the surface; it is made up of several large groups of compact cells referred to as the basal ganglia. These neurons are known to have a great deal to do with regulating the co-operative efforts of groups of muscles, especially in relation to the adjustment and maintenance of body posture.

Think for a moment of the movements of anyone playing an instrument. Not only are the fingers moving, but the upper muscles of the arm are also holding the hand in a position so that the fingers can do their job. No matter what else is going on in the body, whether it is standing still or moving, it remains necessary for the brain to control the relationship between the hands, and often the mouth, and the musical instrument.

A good way to visualize this process is by imagining that you are playing the violin, your left hand turned palm-up, the forearm rotated, and the fingers partially flexed as they would be to depress individual strings of the instrument in order to control their length.

Now imagine instead that you are holding a saxophone. To do this, and to depress the keys that adjust the length of the air column in the instrument, you will have had to rotate your hand 90 degrees, to a thumb-up position. Finally, put yourself at a keyboard, and notice that you must now rotate your hand yet another 90 degrees to a palm-down position, so that your fingers can depress the keys of the instrument.

You haven't played a note yet, and all this prearranging has had to take place, selecting shoulder, elbow, and wrist angle and rotation, and presetting muscle tone in the upper body appropriate to the particular instrument you will be using. Happily, despite its complexity, this is a part of the process that is organized unconsciously.

How is this done? First, and most important, it has been confirmed that neurons in the basal ganglia can activate muscles, in the same manner as has been described for neurons in the motor strip of the cortex. However, they appear to do this indirectly, sending their instructions to the spinal cord and muscles *through* the neurons located within the motor strip. In this way the basal ganglia can assist higher centers by arranging groups of muscles into a body posture appropriate to the intended task. It was thought until recently that this was a subsidiary or background role, and that the basal ganglia had little to do with the specific control of *distal* components of skilled movements (e.g., finger movements). More recent work has suggested (as you might have guessed) that things are never as tidy or as simple as one might hope.[5]

If one had to summarize the current thinking, it would seem safe to say that basal ganglia are involved in the initiation of limb movements, including skilled movements, in at least two important ways: first, by linking a motor sequence to environmental circumstances; second, by orienting the distal portion of the limb so that it can effectively interact with an external target. It is as though the responsibility of the basal ganglia were to ask three questions before any move: (1) What are you planning to accomplish with these movements? (2) What tools are you planning to use? and (3) What are things like where you are planning to do all this? With the answers to those questions, the best muscular or body "set" for the job can be arranged ahead of time. When that has happened (which probably eats up a few hundredths of a second) the basal ganglia say, in effect, "Let's go!"

We now come to the third component of the motor control system, the cerebellum. Nested underneath the hemispheres, at the base of the brain, this massive structure is perhaps the most enigmatic of all neurologic structures. Although its size and connections suggest a major role in motor control, its full range and method of operation remain a mystery. This much is clear: It works closely with other elements in the system to improve the smoothness and timing of muscular contractions—obviously two aspects of performance critically important for musicians.

Current theorists accept a longstanding separation of functions which correspond roughly to its anatomical subdivisions. The older, midline part is intimately connected to the structures in the brain and ear responsible for balance (the vestibular system), and if you knock this part out, your days with the ballet company are over. My pianist friend who plays on cruise ships would be in serious trouble without this part of the brain (I said this to him once, and he replied that he was in trouble anyway).

The intermediate cerebellum has been known for quite a long time to be concerned with what is called feedback, or current control of muscle activity. When you reach for something, the initial muscle contractions that launch the limb are under the guidance of basal ganglia and motor strip, working together. They produce a sort of first-approximation fling of your arm and hand toward whatever you are reaching for.

Once the limb is on the way, joint, tendon, muscle, and skin receptors give a continuously updated set of progress reports on the movement of the limb, which can be supplemented by visual tracking. It is the intermediate cerebellum that is interested in all this information. It wants to see how well you are reducing the discrepancy between where you are and where you want to be, and to assist its colleagues in adjusting the trajectory when that is necessary.

Because of this finely tuned collaborative network, we are able to carry out a virtually limitless variety of motor tasks, smoothly and skillfully, sometimes under novel environmental conditions. The next time you watch a juggler on a unicycle, balancing a bowling pin on his nose, you will know you are in the presence of someone whose cerebellum is in top condition.

Dr. Gordon Holmes, a pioneer scholar of cerebellar function, noted some years ago that cerebellar malfunction leads to characteristic difficulties: You are still able to reach out, grasp, and manipulate objects, but the quality of muscle synergy is disturbed.[6] Alcohol, to which the cerebellum is remarkably sensitive, exerts its earliest crippling effects on tap dancers, musicians, and night owls by inactivating this part of the motor system.

Recent motor system research has begun to open our eyes to the importance of the largest subdivisions of the cerebellum, its lateral portions. The major impediment to interpreting lateral cerebellar contribution to motor control stems from its unique wiring, which precludes it from assisting the intermediate cerebellum with the feedback modification of ongoing movements. Most of its conversation takes place over the back fence: It seems to talk only to the neurons in or near the motor strip. For the most part, it has no way of knowing how well any movement may be proceeding from moment to moment, so there isn't much it can do to help if things are off track.

Before seeing where neurophysiologists are presently headed with their theories of lateral cerebellar function, we should stop here and take stock of what we have found up to this point. We know enough now to have a rough idea of how the motor system does its job.

First, any movement that is intended has to begin with an idea. The translation of that idea into physical movement calls the entire system into play. A series of coded signals begins in basal ganglia and in the motor strip, and is relayed to the spinal cord. This causes activation of a group of muscles which move the limb toward the intended target. Immediately at the time of movement onset, nerves in the muscles, joints, and skin, and the eyes watching the activity, begin reporting back the progress of the intended move. This permits adjustments or corrections to be made so that the limb can be brought smoothly to its intended target.

Up to this point, the musician is doing exactly what baseball and tennis players are doing, with respect to the general strategy used by the brain to control skilled movements. He is moving selectively in relation to some external object, positioning himself and adopting a posture appropriate to his intentions, and then going through a sequence of moves to alter the behavior of the external object. He has available to him a set of both conscious and unconscious physiologic systems to regulate the muscles being used, and he can make instantaneous corrections in their activity if necessary to avoid missing his target.

It turns out that this scheme is correct, but incomplete. It doesn't explain how the body can make movements of the kind necessary to play 6266 notes in 4 minutes and 20 seconds in the correct order, without error—or even come close. Never mind whether they sound musical or not. When things are happening this fast, there simply isn't time to get information back and forth in the nervous system fast enough to make corrections if the move isn't on target. So there has to be another way to explain how the brain manages to accomplish this task.

The first important clue to understanding the control of these moves was discovered almost ninety years ago. In 1895, Paul Richer took a series of rapid-sequence photographs of the quadriceps muscle during a kicking motion. After studying the photographs, he said this about the contraction of the muscle during the kick: "It is very energetic and short lasting. It launches the limb in a set direction and ceases long before the limb will have completed its course of action." Because of the similarity of this kind of move to the firing of a gun shell, it was called "ballistic."[7]

It is now recognized that highly skilled movements, particularly those that are rapidly executed and brief in duration, are under the guidance of a far more complex control system than is required for movements which can be corrected by ongoing adjustment, or so-called current control. It must be emphasized that the movements themselves need not be shotlike to come under the ballistic mode of control. The essential characteristic of the control system is that the details of the movement must have been completely worked out in advance, in a lengthy trial and error process, so that the movement can be executed when it is called for with absolute accuracy, each and every time, in a nearly automatic way. This means that the brain, or the motor control system, must issue in advance of the move an ordered series of command signals that specify what the muscles involved must do, from start to finish, before the movement itself actually begins. Since there is no time to correct mistakes once the move has begun, everything must be right from the very beginning.

This is a bit like what happens when you use your own long distance telephone company to call someone. You punch in all the numbers ahead of time, instructing a group of complex switching devices scattered all over the country to organize each other so that your friend's telephone will ring, and when the phone is picked up your voice will be heard. All those signals and all that equipment will just sit there until you hit the last number, completing the program for the entire ballet.

At the present time, it is not clear how the development of the ballistic mode of control comes about. Most experimental studies suggest that a shift from conscious, deliberate (and relatively slow) control to fast, unconscious control will occur whenever short movement sequences are repeated frequently under circumstances when speed and accuracy are important.

The cerebellum, and particularly the part of the cerebellum called the lateral hemispheres, has been proposed recently as the part of the brain mainly responsible for permitting us to develop these highly skilled, automatic (ballistic) movements. One finds a certain amount of computer language in discussions of this subject; for example, it has been suggested that the lateral cerebellum can be thought of as the home of a set of subprograms of movement, where the software critical to the accurate and smooth performance of highly rehearsed movement operates.[8]

All this sounds very promising, but we will still be guessing about the details until someone figures out a way to make the appropriate measurements of electrical activity in the brain and muscles of a musician during live performance.

Advance programming of skilled movements is one important feature of ballistic control. Another equally significant feature is the striking change in muscle responsiveness that occurs in this condition. The physical fluidity which a performer enjoys when he or she is "on," or is playing "unconsciously," almost certainly stems from a marked shift in the physiologic behavior of muscles coming under a ballistic mode of control.[9]

The experienced musician may actively seek an inner state during performance in which the muscles feel warm, relaxed, and light, and use that feeling along with auditory information to confirm that things are going well. Do you recall the earlier discussion of *inhibition* of contraction? It could well be that one of the major functions of the cerebellum is to oversee this critically important aspect of skilled movement, by targeting "turn off!" messages to neurons elsewhere in the motor system, and sequencing them just as precisely as the "turn on!" messages that get things going.

Think for a moment what happens when a performer loses confidence and begins to worry about the mechanical details of execution. Movements immediately slow down, the muscles become stiff, and it isn't long until (as expressed in a famous rock and roll hit) there's "a whole lotta shakin' goin' on!"

We have one remaining technical matter to consider. You will recall that with ballistic movements the instructions had to be worked out in advance. Although this advance programming works very effectively, it presents one important drawback: No two pianos are the same, and keys and valves occasionally stick on the best pianos, trumpets, and horns. In other words, we live in an untidy and changing world, and the amount of muscular contraction needed to accomplish a specific task may vary considerably depending on the circumstances in which the job is carried out. Furthermore, the mechanical properties of the muscle itself may change for a variety of reasons. For example, when the hands are cold the muscles become stiff and do not contract as quickly as when they are warm. Ask any kid in a high school marching band that does half-time shows for nighttime football games. No matter how carefully the signals have been worked out in advance, it's no good if the instrument doesn't behave or the muscles are not responding normally. In the case of extreme conditions or muscular fatigue, it doesn't matter what the signals from the brain dictate: Performance is not going to be the same as usual.

Astonishingly, even this problem seems to have been anticipated and provided for in the engineering of our neuromuscular system. Each muscle employs a microscopically small sensing and control system, consisting of what are called muscle spindles, imbedded in the muscle, and a self-contained reflex subsystem located in the spinal cord which can act directly on the anterior horn cells. Because of this system, the muscle can make instantaneous adjustments in its response to control signals coming from the brain, according to conditions in the muscle at the time the orders from headquarters arrive. In a real sense, the spindle system works in the same way the small computer worked on board America's first lunar lander, the *Eagle.* In the final seconds of that landing, when the lag in radio transmissions made it impossible for the computers at the space center on Earth to solve the final landing control problems, the small computer on board the capsule took over the job. The same thing happens when a finger playing a fast passage hits a key or a valve offering unexpected resistance—the pressure necessary to correct the touch will be computed by the spindle mechanism, the muscle force will be corrected, and an uninterrupted, smooth performance will be the result.[10]

We have now reached a zenith of sorts. We started with the description of a mechanism which keeps us on our feet going downstairs, even if the stairs are on a ship plunging through a typhoon. We saw that there is a reason we can drive cars, open doors, drink beer or tea, tie our shoelaces, and ski down mountains, more or less without mishap, even though each of these events is largely novel in its detailed execution every time we do it. Finally, we found that when we want to learn to do something very fast, smoothly, and without mistakes, and do it automatically, we can do *that* too. All it takes is work; complex skills and absolute reliability demand more time and greater concentration during the learning process, but the potential for improvement is still a property of the wiring. Virtuosity is no big deal, if you don't mind practicing.

What we have not surmounted is that last half inch it would take for us to be able to peek over the top. Although much of what is accomplished in finished musical performance is automatized, no two performances are ever the same. Music, it is said, is not a reproduction but a re-creation. So there must be room for instantaneous changes in control, that mysterious, individual, and unpredictable body English that is brought into play no matter how well rehearsed and learned any piece might be. This incredible flexibility of control, in which resides the possibility of making music out of movement, and making it fresh and alive, is an attribute of the system as a whole—it belongs to the musician. The chances of finding it are about the same as the chances of finding out where they keep flight hidden away in an airplane.

Notes

1. J. Hughlings Jackson, "On the Anatomical and Physiological Localization of Movements in the Brain," *Lancet* (1873), 1:162.

2. Ragnar Granit, *The Purposive Brain,* Chapter 8 (Current Ideas on Brain Control of Movement), MIT Press, 1977.

3. Homer Smith, *From Fish to Philosopher,* Little, Brown and Co., 1953, pp. 195–6.

4. W. Penfield and T. Rassmussen, *The Cerebral Cortex of Man,* Macmillan, 1950.

5. M. Delong and A. Georgopolis, "Motor Functions of the Basal Ganglia," in *Handbook of Physiology: The Nervous System,* American Physiological Society, 1981, 1017–1061.

6. Gordon Holmes, "The Cerebellum in Man," *Brain* (1930), 62:1–30.

7. Paul Richer, "Note sur la Contraction du Muscle Quadriceps dans L'Acte de Donner un Coup de Pied," Société de Biologie Comptes Rendus (Paris), 1895, 47:204–205.

8. V. Brooks and W. T. Thach, "Cerebellar Control of Posture and Movement," in *Handbook of Physiology: The Nervous System,* American Physiological Society, 1981, pp. 877–946.

9. L. D. Partridge, "Muscle Properties: A Problem for the Motor Controller Physiologist," in *Posture and Movement,* eds. R. Talbott, D. Humphrey, 1979, pp. 189–229.

10. P. Matthews, "Developing Views on the Muscle Spindle, Spinal and Supraspinal Mechanisms of Voluntary Control and Locomotion," in *Progress in Clinical Neurophysiology,* 8, ed. W. Desmedt, 1980, pp. 12–27.

4

Did You Hear What I Just Heard?

LISTENING WITH THE EARS

The scene is an office building, the time is early evening. Riding down the elevator together are two psychiatrists, whose appearance is strikingly different. The younger of the two is pale, bedraggled, and depressed. The older stands erect, looks crisp, fresh, and happy. The younger man speaks.

> YOUNG PSYCHIATRIST: Jim, I don't see how you do it. How can you listen to your patients all day long and look the way you do now?
>
> OLD PSYCHIATRIST: Who listens?

Doctors are fond of jokes playing on the distinction between hearing and listening. So are musicians. In one of the countless sublime routines he recorded, Victor Borge mentioned his twins, admitting sheepishly: "I can't remember their names. Oh well, it doesn't matter—they don't come when I call them anyway."

The goal of this and the succeeding chapters on auditory perception is to acquaint you with the basic design and operation of the sound-processing equipment you now own and use, whether or not you are a musician. It is not an easy subject to explore casually, as it has become the focus of attention and active investigation by a number of scientists interested in sound and our responsiveness to it. The challenge to the student is made greater by the sheer number of disciplines involved: It includes psychologists, neurophysiologists, neurologists, otolaryngologists, acousticians and psychoacousticians, linguists and psycholinguists, and, of course, advertising agencies. Certainly the last of these groups seems to know what it's doing. If they can make their way through all the smoke, so can you. Be brave.

If the state of our own hearing is such that we can pass a screening test, we consider ourselves fortunate and regard the matter closed. If we can't hear what musicians say they hear in music, we shrug it off. Dogs can hear high-pitched whistles, and musicians can tell when a soprano's high C is slightly flat; it's the way they're built. You are in good company if you have always assumed that you have a pair of openings in the side of your head connected to an amplifier and a recorder, and that musicians just have an upgraded hi-fi. If so, you're in for a modest and encouraging surprise.

Most of us started hearing music when we were quite young and as adults are accustomed to its presence at a huge range of ceremonial occasions. When you review the list it seems as though divorce and paying taxes are the only regularly occurring events lacking standard theme music. Considering the constancy of our exposure to music, it is remarkable that we do not become immune to its effects. Something in our makeup creates an insatiable appetite for music, and not only do we fail to tire of it, but we are almost incapable of indifference to its presence. Like it or not, we have proven the psychologists' claim that we ignore the attachment to our own money when we are being serenaded with soothing music (a grocery store without background music is highly unusual in some parts of this country).

Our involvement, even as nonmusicians, is not entirely passive, though. We turn on our favorite FM station to hear music. We buy record albums. We love going to parades with marching bands, and tend to fall in step just a little when one of our kids is in the band passing us. We go to concerts, we go dancing, and we go to the movies (movies would be flat without a musical background).

In short, we are avidly interested in music, and selective in our responses to it. None of this could occur without the ability to detect and process sound information at a high level of refinement. Let me be specific. We recognize the sound of many common instruments. We have the ability to isolate the sound of individual instruments even when they are playing in a large ensemble. One of the reasons we enjoy listening to Prokofiev's *Peter and the Wolf*, for example, is that we look forward to the solos of particular instruments. We may have come to enjoy a particular orchestra or band so much that we regularly buy their albums. We may crave the sound made by one of the members of a particular band just as helplessly as some people crave chocolate (the saxophone of the late Paul Desmond always mesmerized me). There is also the "that's our song" feeling we may have about a special piece played by a specific group. So deeply entrenched in our memory are the fine details of a particular performance of this piece that nothing else can make us respond the way the original does (we may even become fairly hostile toward imitations). All of this may be true even though we have never played an instrument, or sung, and can't read music.

If you simply stop for a moment and reflect on the richness of your own musical experience, you should be prepared to acknowledge that you are already engaged in a remarkable range of complex sound-discrimination tasks without the slightest feeling of strain. It might impress you even further if you were to realize that one of the most complex tasks you ever perform is to *reject* a piece of music because you don't like the way it sounds, or feel you don't understand it.

But despite this compelling evidence of our musical interest, unless we have formal musical training we tend to see ourselves as outsiders; our love of music may be great, but our approach to music is different from that of "real" musicians. Most of us do not buy records or go to concerts intending any sort of analytical reflections about the music. We don't give much thought to the technical details of music we choose for ourselves, either before or after listening to it in live or recorded performance. We just like to enjoy ourselves.

Have we missed anything in this role as spectators? One way to decide would be by recalling programs we have attended. If you were to try right now to remember the last concert you went to, what would you come up with? You almost certainly remember the name of the performer, or the group performing, and if you paid for your own ticket you can no doubt name the titles of some if not all the music that was played. You might be able to recall the melodic lines of some of the music, but it would be remarkable if you could hum the entire program all the way through. Since there must have been some music you liked particularly well, you will probably remember the special feeling you had during that part of the program. You may remember the faces of some of the people you saw, and what they were wearing, and the moods of the audience and of whoever was onstage. If anything really unexpected happened, you probably remember that as well as I remember a concert at which the pianist André Watts was the featured soloist, and during which the housing for the piano's pedals broke off as the piano was being wheeled onstage. I can't recall the music Mr. Watts eventually played after the instrument was repaired (it may have been Beethoven's Third Piano Concerto), but I certainly do remember the sound of the broken pedal housing crashing to the floor.

Of course, this was a particularly entertaining distraction, and for us the focal point for subsequent recollection of a concert experience. Let's take a more normal situation (this is a fabricated but I think realistic composite of an average experience). Imagine that we are going to a concert together, to hear a young woman who will play the guitar. We find ourselves seated in a row with the young woman's husband, next to whom is her teacher, and in the row just in front of us are the music critics for two local newspapers.

As the concert proceeds, we find the program to be enjoyable, with a few minor hitches. She has some microphone trouble early on, which is corrected, and stumbles momentarily during one very fast passage in the second half of the program. We are struck by the evident discomfort of her husband when this happens, the stoicism of her teacher, and the discreet note-taking evident in the row in front of us. At the end of the program, at a small reception held in the lobby, we hear the performer remark confidentially to a friend that she had omitted an entire section of one of the pieces because she couldn't remember it. The friend, also a musician, laughs and chides the guitarist over her concern about the mistakes. "You were absolutely wonderful," she says, and obviously means it. It is not clear that this reassurance lifts the cloud, however. The general mood of the audience following the concert is very positive. Comparing our reaction to that of some of the musicians or critics present, one might conclude that *they* are the ones who missed out on the fun!

Obviously, there are any number of ways a musical program will have meaning for those in attendance, and it is remarkable how varied (and sometimes inconsistent) our impressions of what took place may be. For the musician, musical details seem to assume a prominence in their immediate experience and later recall of the event that they do not assume for the rest of us. The degree to which we are *not* involved in the more technical details of the music itself becomes apparent when we try to remember what happened and discover that these are the least distinct of the memories we tuck away.

The trained musician is not really doing anything exceptional when he notices—and retains—musical details from concerts. You do the same thing every time you go to a play. You probably knew something about the plot before arriving at the theater, and even if your main reason was to see the star, you shouldn't have much difficulty describing what happened, even long after your having seen the play. You at the play, and the musician at the concert, recall these details because the events you are witnessing have meaning for you beyond the simple pleasure you derive from the spectacle.

You are entitled to ask whether it really matters that you understood what was being done. If you were there and had a good time, what difference does it make? Some people at a concert will have had a particular interest in the technical details of the program, and will therefore focus their recall on those aspects of the program of special interest or concern to them. Prior to our guitar concert the teacher, for example, might have worked with the performer on passages that seemed to need technical or interpretive polish, and therefore listened with particular care during the performance of those passages. Others, like the husband or a close friend, were more concerned about the overall effect of the performance, and so were particularly attentive to any signals that things were going well, or badly. The critics, on the other hand, were expected to be knowledgeable about the music, and to be objective reporters of what the guitarist actually did. All these people *should* have had differences in their general impressions of the concert.

Our intuition tells us that everyone at a performance hears the same music, but because certain people have a special point of view, they will respond to the performance in individual ways.

Before deciding happily to "leave the details (and the arguments) to the experts," we really ought to ask once more the question we began with: Do we relinquish anything of value as a result? The answer has great bearing not only on our pursuit of music as listeners but on our motivation and method of study of an instrument for our own pleasure.

The answer, for me, is yes, we do miss something of value. In order to understand why I say this, there are two aspects of listening we need to consider. First, recall the example of the stage play. Your ability to relish the experience after it is over is dependent on your ability to recall a wealth of detail from the performance. Your comprehension of the language (both spoken and unspoken) is what gives you the ability to see beneath the surface events and to appreciate the subtleties of the plot and the intricacies of the personalities and relationships explored through the plot. In other words, you have a highly developed and well articulated frame of reference to use in following and remembering what is presented. Without that, you would have little to do but watch the costumes and people move across the stage, and not much to remember (or think about) afterward.

Recently, a few adventuresome opera companies in this country have made what they feel is an important step in bringing greater audience involvement and appreciation to their productions. They have been using English supertitles which can be seen by the audience during the opera. Response to this change has been interesting: Some old-timers find the addition distracting (these people already know what the opera is about), but newcomers report with some excitement that they can now tell what is actually happening during the performance. A door has been opened to their understanding.

The question for us to consider is this: Would our enjoyment of a musical event be enhanced if we had a structure, like a language, with which to approach it? I will return to that issue momentarily.

My reluctance to "leave the details (and the arguments) to the experts" is based on another conviction, which is very close to the heart of this book. It has to do with the effect of experience and learning on our *physiologic* responses to the world we live in. Let us return for just a moment to the guitar concert. After noting the variety of responses to the music, we concluded that "everyone hears the same music, but because certain people have a special point of view, they will respond to the performance in individual ways." But *did* everyone, in fact, hear the same music?

Let me offer in evidence the following slightly edited quotations from two newspaper reports which followed a concert I attended a little over a year ago. I'm not making this up. Here is what critic number one said:

> Searching for something fresh to say about the Symphony in D Minor may well be impossible, but one can appreciate the fine, resonant, splendidly balanced interpretation that was elicited from the players. The little answering phrases between strings and woodwinds in the first movement, for example, were neatly done, the brass accomplished throughout.

And the second critic:

> During the Franck Symphony in D Minor, the code words were loud, louder, loudest. The conductor waved his hand in the direction of pianissimo every now and again, but nothing came of the gesture. He asked for more sound when the men of the brass section were already red in the face and, worst of all, he let the orchestra play out of tune.

Confronted with a difference of opinion this extreme coming from seasoned observers, we might simply laugh and wonder whether these two critics were really present at the same concert. The discrepancy in their observations on the brass section's performance suggests something more than a casual difference of opinion: Either one of the two was guilty of malpractice, or they heard separate and contrasting fragments of the same performance. In either case, if this is what musical understanding leads to, who needs it?

Perhaps the distinguished American composer Aaron Copland can help us answer our question. In *What to Listen For in Music*, a book entirely devoted to this activity, he argues that the formal study of musical structure is necessary if one is to gain access to all that music has to offer. As he puts it:

> In a certain sense we all listen to music on three separate planes. For lack of a better terminology, one might name these: (1) the sensuous plane, (2) the expressive plane, (3) the sheerly musical plane.

He goes on to explain the differences.

> The simplest way of listening to music is to listen for the sheer pleasure of the musical sound itself. That is the sensuous plane. . . . [At the next level] music expresses, at different moments, serenity or exuberance, regret or triumph, fury or delight. . . . [Finally,] besides the pleasurable sound of music and the expressive feeling that it gives off, music does exist in terms of the notes themselves and their manipulation. . . . The intelligent listener must be prepared to increase his awareness of the musical material and what happens to it. He must hear the melodies, the rhythms, the harmonies, the tone colors in a more conscious fashion. [As a more conscious and aware listener you are] not someone who is just listening, but someone who is listening *for* something.[1]

I think this is as economical a statement of the issue as can be found. Its additional appeal, for me, comes from knowing that he is not advocating a highbrow attitude about music. He is stating simply that the more you know, the more you will hear. Taste in music does not refer to one's ideas about style, but about intent and realization. To use a culinary analogy, the goal is to know enough about French cuisine and hot dogs to enjoy both, and to know when you've been presented a junky crepe or a gourmet frankfurter.

The critics' difference of opinion really isn't a problem at all. You are still free to enjoy the music in any way you choose, and can decide for yourself which of the critics was out to lunch.

I find myself at issue with Copland on one assertion he makes in the first chapter, "Preliminaries," of this fine book. This is how he puts it:

> Certain schools of thought are inclined to stress the value for the listener of some practical experience of music. They say, in effect, play *Old Black Joe* on the piano with one finger and it will get you closer to the mysteries of music than reading a dozen volumes. No harm can come, certainly, from pecking the piano a bit or even from playing it moderately well. But as an introduction to music I am suspicious of it, if only because of the many pianists who spend their lives playing great works, yet whose understanding of music is, on the whole, rather weak.

My disagreement with this argument is twofold. I grant that musical skill guarantees nothing by way of understanding basic principles. Musical performance can be learned in a completely imitative fashion, and in some cases is deliberately taught that way. But the practical necessity to learn something about musical form and content is likely to be much greater for the practicing musician (at whatever stage of advancement) than for the individual who seeks this understanding solely in the interest of music appreciation.

Secondly, the musician engaged in an active process of organizing, shaping, and harmonizing sounds is perforce changing the sound-processing mechanism with which he listens to music. Nothing could be more vivid to me in my own experience than this discovery. Before my first encounter with Mozart, I had played a few of the simpler Chopin Preludes. These pieces involve judicious but regular use of the sustaining pedal, which produces a rich and ringing blend of the melodic line with its accompanying chords. Mozart, by contrast, is dry and crystalline, requiring utmost discretion in the use of the pedal. I found it very difficult to heed the warnings on my use of the pedal because my inexperienced ear kept telling me to use it as I had with the Chopin. Finally my teacher, in exasperation, declared: "Frank, if you can't keep your foot off the pedal I'm going to have to tie your leg to the bench!" The problem was not that my foot was stuck to the pedal; it was that I really couldn't imagine (and accept as correct) the sound produced by leaving the pedal alone. Not until I had labored to create a "Mozart sound" myself could I even detect this difference between his piano music and Chopin's.

This became apparent to me several months later when I was listening to a recording of a Mozart sonata and found myself grimacing and saying aloud: "Too much pedal!" The months of concerted effort to get the fingers to do something for the ear had not only changed the fingers: The ear was growing up, too.

This must be the prospect that grabs us. Can we, through effort, get our ears to grow up? Should we bother? We tend to see ourselves as nonmusical if we are not accomplished in the use of an instrument, or singing, and tell ourselves that we just don't have what it takes. We feel this way even though most of us display considerable interest in music, and sustain that interest through most of our lives.

Most of us would like to widen our experience and increase our enjoyment, and would do so if we really thought there was any hope of success. I propose to you that a better understanding of your own auditory hardware will not only create a strong incentive to make the effort to grow but will also give you an awareness and insight that will contribute enormously to the success and pleasure of the learning process itself.

Ready to plunge?

Notes

1. Aaron Copland, *What to Listen For in Music,* McGraw-Hill, 1957.

5

What's the Pitch?

THE MAKINGS OF A MUSICAL EAR

The well trained musician presents so many skills to marvel at, one is hard pressed to know where to start paying homage. For me, and I think for many others, there has always been a particular sense of wonder at the violinist's or the singer's delivery of just the right notes, one after another in flawless procession. It's not the accurate order I'm thinking of; no, what amazes me is that the notes sound as though they belong just because they're in tune. It's easy enough to see how this is done on a piano—you just punch the right key and you have it. If the tuner has done his work, nobody will complain that you're flat.

Of course I'm slandering the pianists. But there is a point that even they will agree to, and one which I would like us to dwell on. The point is that the musician's sense of pitch must be very keen indeed. Those of us who are not "gifted" musicians have a hunch that it is this special ability to conjure up exactly the right sounds (in their heads and on their instruments) that separates the sheep from the goats. What we would like to know is whether one can acquire this power or whether it is built in, like the color of your eyes.

As it turns out, there is no simple answer to this question, and no complete answer. In the process of attempting at least a partial answer, we find ourselves at the edge of what is really a much larger question—namely, what are the auditory skills required of the musician?

We are just beginning to appreciate that there is indeed something quite remarkable about how the human brain receives and processes sound information. Like other animals, our responsiveness to any vibrations arriving at the ear depends on our interests and needs at the time sound signals enter the nervous system. We have the capacity to respond dramatically to extremely minute changes in the acoustic environment while simultaneously ignoring other changes of enormous magnitude, depending on their immediate importance to us.

Our responsiveness to music, however, like our responsiveness to language, appears to be a different matter, depending on a power of synthesis of auditory and cognitive skills unique in the animal kingdom. Even relaxed listening is an active process, dependent on physiologic mechanisms greatly influenced by previous auditory experience and present intent. Thus, although listening to music may be only a recreational pastime, it is an activity which depends on the exercise of a singularly human neurologic potential, and is never passive.

In this chapter we will introduce the matter of pitch perception (because it is what most people talk about), and then we will cover a few basic facts about sound transmission in the atmosphere and inside the head. Then, in the chapters that follow, we will try to see what the brain has to do with it.

In the wake of an early skirmish with a music teacher, many of us were left at a young age with the impression that we were "tone deaf." In practical terms, this was a reprieve. If at the age of eight or nine one had to be able to carry a tune to be in the chorus, then tone deafness was a disability that could be accepted with dry eyes.

It is interesting to contrast the docility of such a retreat with the probable response of a nine-year-old boy or girl, aglow with baseball fantasies, advised by the coach that "your arm isn't good enough for you to be on the team." You know exactly what this youngster will do with the news that he or she doesn't have "the perfect pitch." Two weeks later the doctor is prescribing ice packs for the elbow!

The trouble with predictions of failure in music is that they normally go unchallenged. They then take a foothold in the mind, as it were, as a rationale for inertia. For most children, a diagnosis of tone deafness becomes the basis of a lifelong conviction that music is out for them. And it is a great loss.

Perhaps the way to begin a reconsideration of this pervasive and powerful misconception is to acknowledge that there are indeed people who seem to lack the necessary equipment to extract musical information from the sounds in the environment. Such people are quite rare. But they are not so much tone deaf as tune deaf. They do not react when you sing "Happy Birthday" because this familiar melody sounds to them no different from any other one might hum or sing. If this is the situation, music would be an unrewarding pursuit.

Recently, a survey was conducted to test the hypothesis that tune deafness is an inherited trait; in their published report the investigators argued that the evidence supports the hypothesis. I have no idea whether their conclusions were warranted or not, but I am grateful to them for reviving the following English limerick to illustrate the problem:

> There was an old fellow of Sheen
> Whose musical sense was not keen.
> He said: "It is odd,
> I can never tell God
> Save the Weasel
> From Pop Goes the Queen!"[1]

What most people mean when they *claim* to be tone deaf is that they are unable to regulate the pitch of their own voice closely enough to match it to a standard. Thus, if shown a note on a musical scale, they would be unable to produce with their own voice the specified pitch. Or, if given a sample sound (another voice, or a note played on a pitch pipe or piano), they would be unable to imitate it vocally. Most of us are unable to do this without formal training, because doing so requires a high degree of control of the muscles which regulate sound production in our vocal tract. If we are unable to burst into song, it is nonsense to criticize our genes; just as with the throwing arm, development of the voice takes practice.

The great majority of people who regard themselves as tone deaf do far better at this sort of thing with an instrument whose pitch they *can* control. Thus, it is usually easy for them to find the correct key on a piano if they are allowed to search in a trial and error process. If you believe yourself to be tone deaf and have never tried this, you should. You will most likely be surprised at how quickly you learn to match tones you hear, and at the improvement in accuracy that comes with practice.

A very small number of people will have difficulty even with this task. When their problem is analyzed, it usually turns out that they have trouble determining relative pitch. That is, they will not be able to answer the question, "Which of these notes is higher?" when two notes are being compared—even if the notes are as much as a full tone apart (e.g., C to D). The situation here is not unlike that of the youngster with normal eyes and intelligence who has to struggle with reading.

Although it may be technically correct to consider confusion over relative pitch as a form of tone deafness, the problem might actually be as much linguistic as musical in origin. That is, it may be correct to argue that the problem comes from an inability to assign a quantitatively specific pitch label to a sound we hear. This may seem farfetched, but it really is not. We regard ourselves as having an instinctive color sense (if we are not color blind), yet there is persuasive evidence that this skill is highly developed in our culture because we are taught to label colors at a very early age, and the names we use (green, red, etc.) are always attached precisely and consistently to specific regions of the visible spectrum. That is, we agree on and regularly use quantitative hue labels.

It seems very likely that the same potential capacity for precise and consistent naming of the audible spectrum exists in virtually all of us. It is not capacity so much as experience that we lack when it comes to the use of the meat and potatoes terminology of the musical world. After all, if we are not involved in musical tasks, why should we take the trouble to learn the vocabulary?

For the average person who is musically untrained, it is difficult (no, impossible) to decide what letter-name to attach to a test note that has just sounded (is it a C? is it a G#?). But it is usually not a problem to say that one note should be called high or low, or, in a comparison test, higher or lower. By the use of such labels we establish that we are sorting the tones according to their relative position on a pitch scale. Another way to put it is that we are able to say whether they are above or below one another on a sort of ladder, without specifying which rungs they happen to occupy.

Perhaps the distinction between having the ability to do, and having the language to describe what is being done, would be made clearer by the example of our use of spoken language. The average person is an avid speaker and listener in conversation. He may puzzle from time to time over grammatic niceties, but generally finds the acts of speech and listening to demand very little labor over the weighty problems of syntax and semantics. And never does casual discourse require insight into the acoustic phenomena involved. We don't need to know anything about the frequency range of our voice, or about the modulation of pitch that turns a statement ("*This* is the room") into a question ("This is the *room?*").

Not only would we be at a loss to understand spoken language, we would have great difficulty recognizing each other's voices if we were deaf to the linguistic information imbedded in the fine details of its physiologic adjustment. Beyond this, we use the most delicate pitch and volume fluctuation (accents and inflection) in our own speech to register our feelings, and at times communicate far more this way than we do with the words we use. Remember when you used to apologize for bashing your kid brother, only to have your mom grab your ear and say, "I don't like the *tone* of your voice!" She knew what you meant.

The next time a good friend talks to you on the telephone and you find yourself wondering whether he or she is upset, see if this suspicion doesn't have something to do with the voice sounding slightly higher than usual. We may not be able to tell what key our friend is worrying in, but we have no trouble telling something's wrong.

If you remain unconvinced, there are other simple observations you can make regarding your own responsiveness to subtleties of pitch. Listen to a recording of someone who does voice impersonations. Compare attempts to re-create Jack Benny's famous exclamation, "Well . . . !" One of the reasons we find these routines so funny is that our exquisite sensitivity to the musical characteristics of speech (including pitch) allows us to recognize a personal vocal signature while telling us simultaneously that it's fake.

In sum, the collection of pitch names, or labels, which we personally command neither defines our potential for making these distinctions nor reflects the level of skill we exhibit in a variety of everyday perceptual tasks in hearing. Our facility with these labels only indicates the degree of *verbal* refinement we exercise in making technical descriptions of the sounds we hear. If we become actively involved in music, we may find ourselves becoming highly skilled in our use of this terminology.

It has been an intriguing postulate of psycholinguists for some years that labels and perception are like chickens and eggs—if you have a name for a distinction, you are likely to make it. If it is important for you to see a difference between things that are similar, you will be likely to have separate names for those things. The eminent psychologist Harlan Lane employed an elegant and wonderfully funny inversion of baseball banter to make this point. He called it the "I sees 'em the way I calls 'em" phenomenon. The implication is that musical experience should change our ability to label, which in turn should enhance our ability to perceive. I think that's what was happening with me when I had to undiscover the pedal in my early attempts to play Mozart.

Musical experience obviously has something to do with the degree of refinement we develop in auditory perception, and it is not difficult to demonstrate this. For example, it is commonplace among advanced musicians to discover that they have "perfect pitch" for (or can correctly label notes produced by) their own instruments. A bassoonist hears another bassoon play a single tone and correctly identifies its pitch ("that's an F"). A piano plays the same pitch and our bassoonist is no better off than you or I. Each instrument produces a characteristic mixture of secondary frequencies called overtones, or harmonics, and these provide the musician with the information needed to make pitch judgments about the sounds an instrument makes when it is played. We will explore this matter in greater detail in the next chapter.

The example of the bassoonist introduces another matter about which there is some misunderstanding. Although there is enormous complexity to auditory perception, the idea has made its way around that musicians should have something called perfect pitch—that's what determines whether you will be musical or not. The truth is that the ability to identify a pitch, or to produce a required pitch with precision, can be learned. As with most skills (like typing or hog-tying), some people get it faster and possibly better than others. A few musicians have what seems to be an innate sense of pitch, which is usually called absolute pitch, present from early childhood and often discovered by accident (i.e., they didn't struggle over it and may have been surprised to learn they had this ability). These people are not all that common, and as musicians they may end up feeling cranky a good deal of the time since almost everything but their own playing usually sounds out of tune to them.

I do not mean to reject the claim that there are people who are tone deaf, or tune deaf, or otherwise restricted from certain kinds of musical experience. There are, in fact, a number of genuine disorders of the auditory system which can diminish responsiveness to music. But these problems occur so rarely that they do nothing to advance the claim that most people are tone deaf. In any case, there is considerably more than pitch perception involved in musical perception, and most people fail to utilize their capacities in musical tasks simply because of inadequate training. Whether this lack of experience actually reduces ultimate potential is a fascinating question, in my opinion unresolved at this moment, and in any event of no practical concern to the recreational musician. Just developing what you *do* have should keep you pleasantly occupied, and more than slightly amazed when you discover what you weren't hearing before.

We are now ready to tackle a bit of neurophysiology. In order to introduce some of the more remarkable features of the human auditory system, let me tell you of an instructive experience I had one day with the family cat. I was enjoying a quiet weekend afternoon in the back yard, and observed the cat in a state of intense concentration, watching for movement in a patch of ground cover. She was doing what cats seem to do best—being patient and attentive. As I watched her, I felt an impulse to see whether I could sneak up behind her unnoticed. If I could tag her before she heard me, I would be the winner. My wife calls this kind of game "teasing the cat," and I don't think she understands how much the cat looks forward to it.

So I set out on all fours, slowly creeping toward the unsuspecting cat. She remained preoccupied with her own plans, unaware that she was no longer just predator but prey. Well, that's an old game in the jungle, where cats come from, and it's hard to beat them at it. The moment I got close enough to tag her, her ancestry asserted itself.

In the space of a second or two she uncorked an impressive chain reaction to the discovery of my presence. I think it had four distinct components. First, she jumped. This instantaneous contraction of her body seemed the immediate and probably involuntary physical response to the sound of what must have seemed a very near threat. Second, still airborne, she turned to see what was behind her. This maneuver placed her in a position to see what had made the unexpected sound and at the same time to adopt a defensive posture which would not have to be rearranged much after she landed. Third, solidly planted on the ground, she arched her back and hissed. This gesture was obviously meant to signal that I had chosen the wrong kitty to mess with. Then she relaxed; she recognized me.

I had set off the general alarm, unleashing a preprogrammed physiologic survival system. As soon as she recognized me, the whole works was uncocked. The change in her facial expression was sublime: "It's that fool again; I wonder what it's like to live with normal people?"

I cite this small encounter because it will be helpful as a reference point in the following discussion about the human auditory system. If we make it through this, I think you will share my view that tone deafness and perfect pitch are interesting but only peripheral issues related to our responsiveness to music.

The fundamental job of the auditory system is to *detect* sound. This was what the cat was doing as the first part of her discovery of my intrusion into her sphere. She did not need to know who or what I was—just that I was there. The second job of the system is to *locate* the source of the sound. The exceedingly brief time she was airborne was more than sufficient for her to determine the direction from which the noise had come, and to modify her basic landing routine so that she would end up with head and eyes looking straight at the source of the sound, torso and legs set in a preparatory defense posture.

The third job of the system is to *identify* the source of the sound, as a prelude to selecting the appropriate interaction with that source. In the case we are discussing here (cat = 1, neurologist = 0) there wasn't much of a clue in the noise I had made to indicate who I was. It was a twig that had snapped, but what had hit the twig? Because of her maneuver she was able in very short order to secure the necessary visual information to determine that she was in no danger.

The auditory system has built into it a set of high-priority and fast-acting connections to other parts of the brain which function together in a reflex manner. We have almost no ability to modify the operation of this system. Indeed, having the whole thing "hard-wired" constitutes a basic safety provision—flexibility would be a luxury adding enormously to the amount of time required to mobilize the body for self-defense in an emergency.

Unfamiliar or unexpected sounds first entering the system are like visitors to the White House, or travelers in airports these days—they have to get through security first. I am repeatedly reminded of the truth of this fact in my own home. My wife is by now quite familiar with the sound of my voice and my footsteps. Yet she still jumps (and often screams, briefly) when I come unseen into a room where she is working. There is little such a person can do to suppress this startle reflex, which may cause them occasional embarrassment. But there are compensations: This sort of person makes an ideal companion for the annual Halloween visit to a haunted house.

Fortunately for us all, the auditory system is much more flexible in its behavior after the first few milliseconds of the security check. Its connections to the rest of the brain develop slowly, over a period of years, and its influence on more complex behavior tends to be a highly individual matter. This arrangement brings us to the fourth and most challenging task of the auditory system, namely to *integrate* incoming sound information with ongoing brain processes involved in adaptive and purposive behavior. On this, the summit plateau of neurologic function, the auditory system is operating outside the domain of simple reflex and contributing to general cognition. At this level of neurologic function, we simply have to give up trying to explain auditory perception by any identifiable neurologic operations, or thinking in terms of the isolated influence of a specific sensory modality (such as hearing, vision, or touch). No one has the slightest idea what happens to the brain when you supply it with Mozart sonatas, Tibetan chants, or the Gettysburg address.

Before we move inside the head, it might be a good idea to be sure that we have a few elementary ideas about sound in proper condition. First, and not to be tricky, there really is no such thing as a sound in the same sense that there are things that we hear (like fire engines and waterfalls). Although we refer to an audible vibration as a sound, when we examine the details we discover that we are really looking at an interaction between the vibration and a living observer, who detects and makes judgments about it. As we will discover, there really is no such thing as pitch either, for the same reason. But we'll wade into that thicket later.

Whenever anything moves, so long as it is not in a vacuum, it will cause the air in contact with it to move as well. When the air in the immediate vicinity of our fire engine moves, it causes a pressure wave to spread outward in all directions, like the ripples when you drop a pebble into the pond. This reaction is produced by the same "I can't move unless that guy moves" principle that works in theater lines, or railroad yards. Think of those long lines of box cars that make up freight trains. When one car moves, the others connected to it have to move more or less the same amount and in the same direction, in rapid succession. That's how sound travels, too. In the air, any molecules moved by the object in motion will transmit that same motion, or vibration, to their neighbors, who will do the same to theirs, and so on.

In telling you about my experience with the cat in the back yard, I mentioned that my intended ambush was thwarted by the intervention of a twig. Its movement was broadcast more or less instantaneously to the air column in contact with her eardrum, causing *it* to move, following which she put on the little demonstration I described to you.

The only reason she refrained from a full-fledged counterattack was that her ears are not just decorations. A few hundredths of a second after her eardrums were set in motion, the entire auditory (and with it her general cognitive) system came into play. We'll get to that story in the next chapter.

The eardrum, like the air that rests against it, moves passively in response to pressure changes at its surface. This means its movements will follow any fluctuations in air pressure to which it is subjected, within the limitations set by its own physical characteristics. For example, if a vibrating object next to the ear is moving back and forth 5 times per second, the eardrum will do the same. If the object happened to be a tuning fork constructed to vibrate at 256 cycles per second, the eardrum would do the same. It would follow any such pattern of vibrations up to a rate in excess of 20,000 cycles per second.

At this point, at the level of the eardrum, what we have is a membrane that responds to changes in air pressure next to the body. How does the brain find out about this? The next step in the struggle of these minuscule air waves to gain the status of a sound occurs just inside the eardrum. Here, there are three small bones (malleus, incus, and stapes), or ossicles, which form a flexible bridge to conduct sound vibrations between the eardrum and a structure called the cochlea. It is the job of the cochlea to turn mechanical energy into electrical energy. This transformation is necessary because the brain itself is completely insensitive to mechanical vibration (although someone in the throes of a hangover might argue about this). The brain, in its role as a biologic computer, requires that all the information provided to it be in the form of electrical impulses. This is just the reverse of what happens in your kid's stereo system. There, electrical impulses are used to drive an element in the speaker cone so that it moves back and forth in the air. The resulting mechanical vibrations in the air seek you out wherever you may be and drive *you* right out of the house.

The cochlea is a snail-shaped structure about the size of the fingernail on your little finger, and there is one located in each of your ears. Curled up inside it, floating in a special fluid, is a thin band of tissue (the basilar membrane) which anchors a collection of structures called hair cells. Each of these cells (there are about 15,000 of them in each cochlea) has the capacity to generate electrical signals, and most of the time they are doing this in a leisurely way, at the rate of one or two blips per second. The signals are transmitted to a part of the brain which has been reserved as a receiving station for auditory information.

A tuft of hairs sticks out at the top of each cell, projecting into another membrane that covers the entire array of hairs, holding them in position. Vibrations conducted through the middle ear by the ossicles are carried to the fluid holding the basilar membrane, causing isolated portions of it to vibrate. And any hair cell attached to a moving portion of the basilar membrane will in turn be set in motion (not unlike tall buildings astride a lively section of an earthquake fault—if you live in California you know what that's like).

Any deflection of a hair cell will influence its firing rate—if the hairs are pushed even slightly in one direction, the rate of electrical firing decreases; if they are pushed in the opposite direction, the rate goes up. Each hair cell works like a telegraph key, and it faithfully sends a message every time the membrane underneath it is set in motion.

Because of its construction, the cochlea is able to do two remarkable jobs. The first, as I have already mentioned, is to convert the energy generated by air pressure waves to electrical impulses which can be transmitted to the brain. The second is to organize all these vibrations to help the brain figure out where they came from. We need to have a practical system for sorting out the vibrations made by the ice cream man from those made by a falling tree, and we have to be able to do this even though the sounds they make arrive simultaneously—we live in a noisy world, inhabited by people and things that move around more or less at will and without regard for whose turn it is to serenade your ears.

It turns out that one of the ways people and things signal in an individual way is the frequency (or frequencies) with which they vibrate. This is enough of a handle for the cochlea to initiate the identification process.

To use a familiar example, if you stretch a rubber band between two fingers and pluck it, you can see it moving back and forth and hear a characteristic sound. Whatever that sound is, it reflects a fairly stable rate of back and forth movement, or oscillation, of the strand of rubber. If you keep up this plucking without changing anything else you will note that the sound and the rate of oscillation don't change much. That's because the physical properties of the rubber band (its size, length, and tension) determine the rate at which it moves back and forth. If you stretch the rubber band a little more, you will notice that it seems to vibrate faster, and it gives off a somewhat higher pitch. Anything that affects the physical state of an object will tend to alter the rate at which it vibrates. The universe, figuratively speaking, is just a colossal assortment of rubber bands, each humming in its own way, and modifying its vibration in ways that reflect its physical state and behavior.

Now, back to the cochlea. How does it use frequency information to help you figure out where all that humming is coming from? The arrangement of hair cells in the basilar membrane does this trick, in the following way. The mechanical vibrations of the eardrum are carried by the ossicles to the cochlea through the up-and-down movement of the stapes bone. Possibly because of its shape, possibly because of the internal acoustics of the cochlea, sound waves at a particular frequency always seem to land on the same small section of the basilar membrane. This means that sound waves of a given frequency always end up causing the telegraph signals to come from the same set of hair cells. In effect, the arrangement is like setting up an assortment of tuned antennas, each of which picks up just one frequency.

To get a feel for how this system might operate, it would help to get some hands-on experience with a system of tuned antennas. If you have a piano, you're in business.

What we wish to show is that an object that tends to vibrate exclusively at one frequency (which is what each hair cell seems to do) will tend to be a sensitive detector of vibrations of the same frequency that happen to wander by. If the unknown object that interests us always hums the only frequency our antenna is listening for, that antenna will announce the arrival of our visitor, each and every time it comes around. In a moment we'll take up the problem of how the antenna does its announcing. First let's see the detection system in action.

We'll use your piano. Let's take middle C, which vibrates maximally at 256 cycles per second. It also vibrates at twice that rate, or 512 cycles per second (this is one of its naturally occurring overtones, or harmonics, and happens because the string can't help vibrating in simple multiples of its natural frequency). Because of the occurrence of this overtone, any string on the piano tuned to 512 cycles per second should come to life when we play middle C.

Play middle C once or twice just to see how it sounds. Notice how quickly the sound dies out (a damper stops the vibration as soon as you release the key). Now do this: Just before playing middle C again, depress the key located one octave higher, pushing the key all the way down and holding it. Do this gently enough so that you don't actually play the note. So long as you hold this second key down, its damper will remain lifted off and it will be free to vibrate. Now play middle C once again by striking that key and releasing it. The lower (and louder) note dies out at once, but you will continue to hear a note one octave higher. The spirit of middle C has seized its companion an octave away (as well as a cohort of hair cells in your cochlea, the nearly tireless sentinels dedicated to the announcement of visits by 256 cycles and its family of overtones). As soon as you release *its* key, the damper returns to its resting position and the piano becomes quiet again.

To make it clear that the activation of the second string is dependent on the specific frequency at which the first string vibrates, keep holding the upper C key down, only now strike the note just *below* middle C. Does the open string an octave above middle C still sing for you? Now try the white key just *above* middle C—the open string is still out to lunch! The two notes adjacent to middle C (B and D) vibrate at frequencies just below and just above 256 cycles per second, and that small difference is enough that their own harmonics do not match the 512 cycle excitation requirement of this octave of middle C. Therefore it cannot act as an "antenna" for either of those notes.

Let's get back to the cochlea, and the hair cells. Because of the behavior of the basilar membrane, each hair cell acts just like one string in the piano. Each one is tuned to respond *only* to a specific and narrowly limited segment of the whole range of frequencies passing through the cochlea. Since these cells transmit their messages to the brain, we have a mechanism that could very well give the brain the system it needs to set up a fingerprint (actually a frequency print) file on things and creatures that go bump in the night. That is, we have a physiologic way to categorize (and hence to recognize) them.

There are a few remaining points about the special features of our sound-detection system that need to be made before we venture into the brain. We have noted that our system permits us to impose a sorting system on the mixture of frequencies that make their way to the cochlea. There are other characteristics of these pressure waves which we must also consider. First, they have intensity, or energy. Waves at the beach have the same characteristic. They may come in at a rate of five each minute (which is their frequency), but some of them may be a foot high and some may be ten feet high. The higher they are, the more energy they contain (and the more they appeal to kids with surfboards). The amount of energy contained in sound waves can vary considerably, and when sounds are mixed together, we also tend to sort them out according to their intensity. There are at least two ways we use intensity differences to help us process sound information. First, they help us judge how close or distant a sound source is. Second, we can use this information to help us locate a sound source to our left or right. Remember the encounter with the cat, who had to work out the geometry of her landing with nothing more than a twig snap to go on. How was this done? In essence, she was able to take advantage of a very slight difference in the intensity of the sound arriving at each ear, which translated very precisely and very quickly to the calculation that the sound could have come from only one place to have been just that much louder in one ear than the other. People seem to do the same thing, and can interpret time-delay information as well. A sound impulse coming from one side of your head is not only louder on that side; it also gets to the ear on that side sooner than to its mate.

Because of the physical properties of high- and low-frequency sound waves, we use different strategies to localize them. Low frequency waves have about the same intensity at the two ears, no matter where they came from, and high frequency waves arrive at about the same time (i.e., have no discernible phase difference) no matter where the source. Consequently, starting an octave or so above middle C, we rely on intensity differences to determine the direction from which the source came, and we use time (or phase) differences for lower notes.

As if all of this were not complicated enough, it turns out that we have a mechanism in the middle ear which allows us to adjust intensity (or volume) by altering the efficiency of the bridge mechanism between the eardrum and the cochlea. A muscular attachment to the eardrum (called the tensor tympani) and another to the stapes (the stapedius) can reduce the intensity of transmission when sound pressure levels are high. It is not clear whether this arrangement has any influence on sound localization, but it is most assuredly a help when the kids are home.

Finally, sound pressure waves have duration. That is, they start and they stop. Sound duration is not easy to measure, since the dissipation of a sound may be very gradual compared to its onset. Tap a bell, or a chime, and you'll see what I mean. This is worth bearing in mind in relation to music, because although musical notation generally specifies the length of time a particular note is to be held, the instruction is not an easy one to honor. Even if this could be done as precisely as a composer might wish, it is absolutely impossible to control the length of time a listener will believe he can still hear a sound he has been listening to. More of this and other "listener supplied" effects in the next chapter.

It is worth mentioning that musical instruments differ from waterfalls and fire trucks in at least one way that is very important for the cochlea, and hence for the auditory system as a whole. That is, musical instruments are intentionally constructed so that their output frequencies can be precisely regulated, and can also be varied according to any workable pattern chosen by the musician.

When one hears descriptions of the artistic intent of a composer, the language used often suggests that the work is constructed musically so as to represent an event or to evoke certain feelings. However earnest this goal may be, the subjective appeal of a piece of music rests in important ways on the physical and physiologic principles governing the interaction of pressure waves in the air and on the detection/analysis system of the listener. This isn't as cold as it sounds. It means that music is worth very little if people can't react to it. It also means that taste in music may have something to do with neurophysiology. This is not a new idea, by the way. But it is now possible to be more objective in discussing the issue, and to devise ways to explore its ramifications. In the process, a remarkable and somewhat surprising alliance between the arts and sciences may be in the making. Although composers have not traditionally thought of themselves as experimenters in auditory physiology, in a certain sense this is exactly what they are. Modern composers of electronic music, who have the power to specify completely the makeup of a sound signal, understand this in a way that very few people realize.

Notes

1. H. Kalmus and D. Fry, "On Tune Deafness (Dysmelodia): Frequency, Development and Musical Background," in *Annals of Human Genetics* (London, 1980), 43:369.

6

That Sounds like Music

What happens to the sound-generated impulses that make their way into the brain itself? That's an enticing and enormously difficult question. Any number of highly resourceful and energetic scientific investigators devote their entire professional lives to the pursuit of an understanding of the workings of the auditory system, and we can do little more here than suggest the excitement of that pursuit.

As a prelude to this discussion, I declare my intention to trifle with, and then abandon, an attempt to explain what music is.* I do so without the slightest sense of discouragement. Never mind that the scientists are unlikely ever to figure it all out, or that the theorists remain at a loss to tell us what we're actually doing when we are making music.

In order to make any sense out of what is to follow, you will have to know just a little about brain research. The quest for an understanding of brain mechanisms in auditory perception is part of the long history of man's curiosity about his own inner workings.

I do not know that there is an officially acknowledged forefather of modern-day neuroscientists, but I suspect it was a caveman. He performed the prototype experiment for all subsequent investigations into the relation between structure and function in the brain by noting that a club applied briskly to the occiput

*My hunch is that it is somehow tied in with antigravity, which explains why we're not even close yet.

of a rival would overwhelm the recipient with the urge to sleep.

Modern methods are less crude (and more expensive) but often follow the same general formula. Operating on the assumption that different parts of the brain are specialized to carry out particular functions, one has only to inactivate some region of the brain, note the change in behavior, and assert that "this gyrus does that job." Phrenology, a less rigorous but also less invasive branch of this same investigative tradition, made the same kinds of correlations based on the feel of the surface of the head. A prominent bulge was thought to betray the presence of a highly developed brain center (and hence potential) for a certain kind of activity.

In the 1860s, this passion for localizing function in the brain was given a powerful boost by the discovery that damage to a small area on the left side of the brain could seriously disrupt speech production. Paul Broca, a French physician, noted that patients with remarkably similar afflictions had virtually identical areas of brain damage, and deduced that this area of the brain was a speech center. The publication of his work stimulated an unprecedented interest in, and documentation of, a wide variety of acquired speech and language difficulties which could be shown to result from isolated areas of brain damage.

There is an important reason for alluding to this history. It is worth knowing that much of what is said to be true about human brain function stems from observations of the effects of disease or injury on previously well and normal people. Without what are referred to as Mother Nature's experiments we would not be much further along in our understanding of brain function than we were in the days of the phrenologists. But it is very important to understand that this approach has some serious traps for the unwary, and you might as well know what the biggest one is. To say that a function is disturbed consistently by damage to a localized area of the brain is *not* to say that such an area is the center which governs that function in the normal brain. At best, one can claim that the damaged or lost portion of the brain made a critical contribution to the neurologic processes responsible for the activity in question. It may sound as though this is quibbling, but it isn't. One hears much these days about music being a right brain function, and that there is a music center in the right cerebral hemisphere. This sort of proclamation is the perfect example of a half-baked notion. It has the inviting feel of a valid concept, but is true only in the most superficial way and ultimately an impediment to our understanding.

Permit me to share with you, as a benchmark of wisdom about localized function in the brain, the exchange between a professor of anatomy and a young medical student during a neuroanatomy lab. The professor was Dr. Gerhardt von Bonin, an internationally recognized researcher and authority on the cellular anatomy of the brain. He assisted in the laboratory several afternoons each week, enjoying a chance to teach and philosophize in a relaxed way during his retirement. I was the student. One afternoon, bewildered at my inability to find in our laboratory specimen something called the collateral eminence, I asked the doctor where it was. He peered over his spectacles, inspected the specimen, and replied in the musical tones of a village burgermeister, "Vell, it could be *here,* und it could be *here;* who cares?!"

The more eager we are to understand specific brain mechanisms in complex behavior, the more cautious we have to be about claims that someone has found a particular mental function to be controlled by one part of the brain or another. When you hear they've figured out where crossword puzzle wizardry, flamenco dancing, or diesel engine repair reside in the brain, it's time to think of Dr. von Bonin and go buy yourself an ice cream cone.

Let us return to the question of how the ear grows up. As we learned in the last chapter, activation of the sound-transducing device in the cochlea leads to the generation of electrical impulses in the upper levels of the auditory system. Because of the internal wiring and switching, messages from each cochlea reach both the left and right cerebral hemispheres. Although we have the capacity to react to sound without the involvement of the cortex, reflex responsiveness doesn't amount to the same thing as hearing. Conscious awareness of sound does not occur unless the impulses reach the part of the brain called the primary auditory cortex, located on the inner surface of the temporal lobe on each side.

Accordingly, my personal requirements for a suitable definition of music include mention of the auditory cortex. Not only is the man with the horn doing something special, but his and our brains must be doing something special in order for his sound to qualify as music. Is it possible to be more specific about the neurologic aspects of this interchange? I think it is.

Music is usually distinguished from other kinds of sound by the organization of its elements into patterns of tones whose frequency, harmonics, timing, and intensity are controlled by the musician. Our tendency to perceive such complex sound *as music* almost certainly depends on the power of the auditory system to process and then compare these separate elements with those of other sounds we have encountered. The "Ah, that's music" judgment must come to us in the manner of other eureka-like experiences ("Ah, Mom's baking bread") when we have enough data to assign incoming sensory stimuli to some sort of class that revs us up. The ear is not equipped to do this job, but the brain is.

The two physical dimensions of sound waves most critical to musicians are frequency and duration. The first concern of the violinist, guitarist, saxophonist, and their colleagues is the realization of a melody consisting of a succession of pitches organized into a rhythmic pattern. There are a number of other ingredients in the sound recipe of enormous importance to composers, artists, and audiences, but for now we must put on blinders and ignore the aesthetics of "good" or "real" music and its creation. We still have to try to understand a little better how the brain decides that some noises go onto the stack labeled music.

I'd like to propose that we approach this problem in the fashion of archeologists, by returning to an old concert and sifting through the ruins. We'll take the guitar recital from a couple of chapters ago and try to re-create our own experiences as observers and listeners. This time, though, we're going to pay closer attention to the dark side of that experience—things that shouldn't have happened, or things that should have happened but didn't. The wrong note, just possibly, is the buried treasure of neuromusicology.

I said in discussing our make-believe guitar concert that the performer had stumbled briefly during one fast passage. How did we come to that conclusion? I am really asking what we heard that struck us as not belonging.

One obvious clue would have been a change in the rate or regularity with which she was playing the notes. Even if she had been playing a piece without any melody ("The One Note Samba" is nearly such a piece) she would have established two important forms of *timing* information for us to use in following her playing. The first of these is tempo, the second is rhythm, and we'll take them in that order.

Almost all music has built into it a set of regularly recurring accents, or beats, which indicate the rate at which the music moves from start to finish. In some cases (like marching music) these are extremely prominent; in others (as in Gregorian chants) they are almost nonexistent.*

---

*If you want to read a more thorough treatment which explores tempo in nontechnical language, I'd suggest Mildred Portney Chase's book *Just Being at the Piano*[1]; we will explore the issue in detail in Chapter 8.

The tempo of any piece of music is a critically important structural element. The composer provides us (through the musician) a reference system with which to follow the movement, or pulse, of the piece, and its melodic events. If there is any variance from this established pulse, we must conclude that it was intended by the composer, or occurred because of an error in play by the musician.

What does this mean physiologically? It means a great deal. First, it means that we have a mechanism for determining and assimilating the rate of movement of the piece from start to finish. We can be synchronized. So quickly and precisely do we do this, in fact, that most listeners know within the first three beats of any piece of music exactly how fast it is going, and can detect extremely small deviations from that rate. In short, we have the equivalent of a clock, which can be set at almost any rate, after which it will tell us when an external timed event we are following is running ahead of or falling behind that rate.

There is something even more remarkable about our sensitivity to the arrival of sounds in timed packages. When we listen to a piece of music, we expect to hear some fluctuation of its pace from time to time. Without this accelerating and slowing of the pace, music tends to strike us as mechanical. Occasionally a sudden change in tempo will occur, but when this happens we have almost invariably been forewarned by a musical signal that the change is intended.

Our ability to detect a disruption in tempo at the guitar recital says as much about us as it does about the performer. Not only do we have a mechanism for precise timekeeping, we anticipate and accept modest variations from the standard, and feel rattled by changes that are unexpected or seem excessive. Somewhere we must have a set of formulas tucked away to tell us how much variation is legal. This is like having a grandfather clock at home with an accelerometer on the pendulum, able to tell us the phase of the moon based on slight fluctuations of the pendulum swing. Deviations from the expected range can even be used to alert us that the sky is falling. That's a fairly sophisticated clock. We'll try to figure out how it works in Chapter 8.

If you would like to get a feel for your own sensitivity to subtle changes in musical pulse (i.e., take your own auditory clock for a test drive), put on a recording of Ravel's *Bolero* and see whether you don't find yourself noticing the tug of its precisely controlled tempo. There was a movie a few years back using this music to accent another sort of tug being felt by a middle-aged adolescent.

Another way we might know that the guitarist had stumbled would be by hearing an unexpected or inappropriate change in the rhythmic pattern of the piece. Although the time pattern of note sequences in almost any piece tends to be quite variable, musical traditions have generally set limits on the degree and character of rhythmic fluctuation to be used by composers in a single work. As listeners, we expect rhythmic variation and find it an important source of appeal in the music, but expect the rules to be followed.

Even though the guitarist will play many rhythmic patterns as she proceeds, our familiarity with music tradition sensitizes us to the kind and degree of variation likely to be encountered. If we happened to be equipped not only with a cultural set of standards by which to follow (and judge) her playing but with a specific recollection of other performances of the same music, we would almost certainly detect mistakes (deviations from the composer's score) that would pass unnoticed by most other listeners. An audience's memory for musical form is material to the success of performance, but can be a heavy burden to the musician having a bad day.

To summarize the matter of timing and our perception of music: We recognize sounds as being musical partly because of the capacity of the auditory system to respond specifically to the temporal patterning of acoustic events; as a consequence, both composers and artists can strongly influence our response to music by manipulating the timing of those events.

We now come to the second musical element that concerns us—frequency. Since we are examining musical shards for clues to our own inner workings, we want to know how else we might have decided that our guitarist had made a playing error. We might have guessed (or known) by recognizing that she had played a note, or several notes, off key (sharp or flat). She might also have played a wrong note. Clearly, in order to have made this discovery we would have to be able to make a conscious separation of sound frequencies.

We have already seen that the cochlea sets the stage for this skill—that's step one. Step two requires this frequency separation to be maintained at the level of the auditory cortex. This is accomplished by the wiring from cochlea to auditory cortex, so that signals coming from particular hair cells always activate the same receiving cells in the primary auditory cortex. By this arrangement, the cochlear map (position is a code for frequency) is faithfully reproduced in the brain. The anatomy of the auditory system thereby exploits the physical acoustics of the external world, and sets you up as the sort of device that can tell whether trains are coming or going, whether the voice at the other end of the phone is your aunt or your uncle, and whether you're listening to a tuba or a trumpet.

In the preceding chapter we considered tone deafness, and touched lightly on the matter of pitch. The intent of that discussion was to convince you that it is entirely possible to have an accurate, high-performance middle ear (able to extract frequency information from incoming sound signals) but be unable to identify a note that is played for you. I would not blame you for thinking that this is a confusing arrangement. If Mother Nature has gone to all this trouble to make you a sensitive and consistent frequency analyzer, why can't you tell what frequency you're listening to? Are you tone deaf, or what?

Remember why the equipment was installed in the first place, before kazoos came on the scene. We needed a way to sort through a constant barrage of sounds to pick out those marking a danger, or an opportunity of specific interest and importance to us. As you may remember from the cat-stalking story, the auditory system begins its work with sound detection. Our survival doesn't usually require that we know what's going to bean us if we don't duck. We just need to move. After that, it may be useful to gather more information so as to identify the source of the sound. Most of the time, of course, we go about this in a leisurely and unthreatened way.

As we saw in the first of these chapters on hearing, we demonstrate a high degree of sensitivity to frequency in our spoken language. We do this quite efficiently and happily without knowing what frequencies we are listening to, or generating, when we ourselves are the speakers. We also listen for car horns, telephones, babies, and teapots, and recognize them because of the frequencies they generate. Even without formal musical training, we can usually tell if there's a real singer in the group when friends gather around a birthday cake—*somebody* in the group can sing on key. We are able to do this so well that we hardly flinch even when all these competing frequencies crowd into the cochlea at the same time.

How, then, do we learn to recognize and name these frequencies? This somewhat tougher perceptual problem almost sneaked past us a few paragraphs ago, concealed in the word "conscious." Responding selectively to sound frequency doesn't demand a descriptive terminology about frequency, or even the knowledge that there *is* such a thing. My cat does this all the time, and she hasn't a clue how she brings it off. Recognizing that sounds themselves have a characteristic denoted by the word *frequency*, even if we're inept at telling frequencies apart (hearing differences, or naming them), means we're up to something only humans are good at. Welcome to step three.

To upgrade our simple frequency analyzer, Mother Nature has taken advantage of a remarkable capacity of the brain, by which it is able to measure and record stimuli whose magnitude can change by extremely small amounts. Put in a nutshell, the strategy is to divide the stimuli into categories and bundles, or "chunks." Any arriving stimulus is weighed, measured, and labeled a member of the category it fits. The stimuli falling within a particular category are there because they tend to produce roughly an equivalent effect. This is just the beginning. The part of the brain that makes up words seems to run a wiretap on the rest of the brain, and when it finds out about these categories, guess what it does? It makes up words for them. Things are never the same after that. It's as though the brain uses words to stand on its own shoulders. The next time you find yourself wandering through the house and are not quite sure why, then hear yourself say: "Keys, what the blazes did I do with the keys," you'll understand why we'd be lost without this versatile system.

This is what happens as a consequence of the auditory system's connections with the rest of the brain. Raw frequency information can be shared with, used, and/or manipulated by other systems, after which all sorts of interesting things can happen. For purposes of our particular interest here, what seems to happen is that the frequency information is separated into perceptually distinct bundles and made available to speech and language areas.

Let me give you a nonauditory example. The range of temperatures in which we feel comfortable is not large. We could easily describe our feelings about temperature with three terms—too cold, fine, too hot. When the caveman's fire became a furnace that was run by a thermostat, technology had come a long way, and it would have been no problem to equip the furnace with a gadget able to measure temperature differences at least as small as a millionth of a degree. One could then ask to have the thermostat set at 68.000517°F or something of the sort. This would be cumbersome all around, and would be a colossal waste of time if you didn't care whether the temperature was 64 or 72.

You know from personal experience how 68°F feels, and unless I miss my guess you can tell the difference between 67 and 68, 68 and 69, and so forth. So you are quite happy to own a thermostat marked with these intervals. This way you can walk into a cold house and get the temperature where you want it just by setting the dial to the spot that gets the temperature to the level you like.

Then there's the familiar example of vision and color perception. We break up the visible spectrum much as we do the audible spectrum, but apply color names to it. According to this system, light energy within one frequency range strikes us as being blue, and that in an adjacent range of the spectrum seems green, and so on.

One of the profoundly important things to know about categorical perception (as this phenomenon is called) is that its use is not restricted to stimuli of a single physical class, or to stimuli we are trying to locate along a simple magnitude scale. Once the word processor gets into the act, categorization is a process limited only by the imagination. In the visual realm, we categorize a good deal more than spectral location (color); we can take shapes of things, like noses, and classify them into those we find attractive, and those that are unattractive, or in any other way that pleases us to consider noses. We can take clusters of facial features that we can distinguish and give them names like Mike, Arlene, or Gramma. We can even take clusters of completed faces and call them things like men, women, or Aztecs.*

Now, what does this have to do with the auditory system? What you may have guessed is that a system like this—a frequency analyzer hooked up with a categorical organizer, sorter, and labeler—is all we would really need to get our ears to acquire a taste for the banjo. Certainly equipment like this allows us to do a whole lot more than just duck when we have to, or to realize that the racket we hear isn't the telephone starting to boil or the baby ringing off the hook. Furthermore, it explains why we detect *frequency* but talk about *pitch.*

We know that frequency is a feature of sound, and that we have no problem extracting frequency from sound and using it. We react to frequency, but we can't hear it. What we hear, and try to locate on a scale, is pitch. Are they the same, or aren't they? You guessed it—they're not. Pitch, a child of the mingling of our frequency detector and the generator of perceptual categories, is what you *decide* you heard. Its relationship to frequency depends entirely on the accuracy of your frequency detector and your experience with sound.

The auditory system appears to use at least two different grouping (or lumping) strategies for classifying frequency information. These seem to take place simultaneously, or at least in very close succession, and both exploit frequency information. The first of these employs frequency information alone, and involves a search for frequencies which are related to one another harmonically.

---

*Believe it or not, not only was the phenomenon of categorical perception recognized in the mid-eighteenth century, its quirky potential for misguiding our perceptions and our thinking was understood. David Hume, in *An Enquiry Concerning Human Understanding,* published in 1748, said this: "A virtuous horse we can conceive; because, from our own feeling, we can conceive virtue; and this we may unite to the figure and shape of a horse. In short, all the materials of thinking are derived either from our outward or inward sentiment: the mixture and composition of these belong alone to the mind and will."

The strategy makes sense because most sounds come from vibrating objects, which must themselves obey the laws of physics when they are set in motion. These laws regulate the manner in which any object of a consistent makeup will oscillate, whether it is a freight train, a piccolo, or a hungry two-year-old.

How about a demonstration. Take an empty wastebasket, hold it above your head, and drop it on a cement floor. Do this a few times and notice what happens. Try something else. You'll get the idea.

Now, if you have one available, go to the piano and play one of the notes a few times. Listen carefully to what you hear. In the case of the piano and the wastebasket, you will have heard a mixture of frequencies which will have given you in each case a sense of *pitch.* That sense of pitch derives from the cluster of frequencies arriving at the primary auditory cortex simultaneously. It is much more distinct on the piano because the piano string was tuned long before you got there, and will give off a clean family of frequencies limited (more or less) to the fundamental, or lowest, vibrating frequency of the string, together with a mixture of overtones or harmonics which are *always the same* for that string (the string didn't invent the laws of physics but has to go along with them).

The analyzer/categorizer in your auditory system has been keeping track of vibrating things since before you were born. When you first opened your eyes and started looking around, you were given the opportunity to connect the sounds of certain things with their visual appearance. You kept records. And on file (somewhere) is the list of naturally occurring harmonics for any given frequency. That's its family. When they all show up at the same time, the auditory cortex concludes that their simultaneous presence is prima facie evidence that a tone of pitch "X" was generated somewhere in your neighborhood. There may be trouble deciding the specific pitch of the wastebasket, however. The wastebasket is so irregular in its makeup that its pattern of oscillation is a jumble. In other words, its frequency/overtone pattern won't sit still for a family portrait.

Even so, your brain has no difficulty at all telling the difference between the wastebasket and the piano. This is due to the second lumping strategy I mentioned earlier, and we'll get to that in a minute. First I want to be sure you grasp the difference between frequency and pitch.

The most potent determinant of pitch sensation created by any sound wave is its loudest audible frequency. The loudest is often the lowest frequency as well, as in the case of a tone produced by playing a single piano key.

The lowest frequency you hear when you strike middle C on the piano is 256 cycles per second. But, as we discovered, the string simultaneously vibrates at a number of faster frequencies (starting with 512 cycles per second). These higher frequencies, or harmonics, form the basic group (or context) in which the most prominent frequency is imbedded. As you listen to the middle C on your piano, your sense of the pitch is dominated by the fundamental frequency and the associated harmonics. When we start to look at this note (with its harmonics) not in isolation but as part of a piece of music, you have to hang on to your hat.

It has been shown in a number of experiments that pitch judgment is strongly influenced by the harmonics present. For example, if the fundamental frequency of a tone is held constant while the frequency of the overtones is artificially raised, listeners will judge the pitch of the fundamental to be rising. In fact, this effect is so powerful that the same thing happens even if the fundamental is *lowered* while the overtones are being raised.[2] Not only that, but it is possible to remove the fundamental frequency itself, and if most of the harmonics are still present, we perceive the fundamental as being present. What is not known is whether this happens because of our memory of the overtone series, or because the basilar membrane ends up vibrating just as though the fundamental frequency were actually present.

I recall recently having a conversation with a music critic who was interested in a technical problem he observed during a symphony concert. The music on this particular evening included Beethoven's Leonore Overture No. 3, during which one of the trumpets plays offstage, to give the effect of a trumpet call in the distance. The critic (a man with long experience as a conductor) had noticed that the sustained note of the trumpet during this particular passage was flat, and had noticed the same error on previous performances of the same piece of music by other trumpet players.

As we discussed his observation (my own ear is not nearly so finely tuned as his, so I had not experienced the note as being flat), we agreed that this "error" by the trumpet player might really be a perceptual illusion. Because he was playing offstage, some of the higher frequencies in the overtone series must have been eaten by the curtain. And the critic, accustomed to this note in the company of its normal harmonics, would have made the astute judgment that the trumpet was generating a note flat in relation to the accompaniment by the orchestra, which was *not* behind the curtain.

This conversation with the critic brings us to the second lumping strategy used by the auditory system for identifying sound sources. This is perhaps the most interesting aspect of human hearing, which figures prominently in the way we respond to music. How did the critic know that there was a single instrument (and in fact that it was the trumpet) which was flat in comparison with the rest of the orchestra? Let's go back to your experimental work with the wastebasket. The question we left hanging at the end of that discussion was this: How is it that your brain can tell the difference between the sound of a dropped wastebasket and that of a piano (played, not dropped)?

You can tell the difference because the auditory cortex can also do another kind of ordering, of the nonsequential kind (like noses, for example), using pitch along with other information. This is the system of grouping or categorizing into what is called timbre. (An aside: The word timbre is French in origin and it means tone quality; it is sometimes pronounced like the first part of tambourine, but if you want to make it sound as though you're talking about trees, that's okay.) However you pronounce it, the word is a tipoff that the concept is exotic; it serves perfectly as an introduction to operations at the highest level of integrated brain function, where it begins to make sense to ask what the human brain and music have to do with each other.

Notes

1. Mildred Portney Chase, *Just Being at the Piano,* Chapter 9 (Innate Rhythm), Peace Press, 1981.
2. R. Plomp, "Pitch of Complex Tones," *Journal of the Acoustical Society of America* (1967), 41:1526–1533.

7

High Altitude Hearing

AUDITORY PERCEPTION ABOVE THE TIMBRE LINE

The word *timbre* captivates musicians, physicists, acousticians, and instrument designers. The concept has always been somewhat romantic, in a way that reminds one of a certain quality of wines denoted by the term *bouquet.* I suspect that a preference for the French label in both cases reflects our homage to a certain uniqueness and refinement of character, and the increase in our sense of mystification as we get to know them better.

In this last of the four chapters on human hearing and its relation to the musical experience, we will look briefly, and rather superficially, at several terms which have become the cherished property of music's most cerebral theorists. *Timbre* is the first of these; *melody* and *tone*[*] are the others.

You should now be sufficiently accustomed to the procedural peculiarities of this book to know that nothing will be settled by this discussion. Questions are not meant to be answered—they are meant to entertain and delight, and to breed more questions. The brain, like music, never fully reveals itself; instead, it continues to invite one to its deeper and more enchanting mysteries.

---

[*]A word of clarification about "tone" is required. When a written note is played, it becomes a musical sound, called a tone. No problem there. The other kind of tone, which we shall hereafter identify with italics, refers to the character or quality of realized musical sound. In order to qualify as a musician, one of the things you're supposed to have is a beautiful *tone.* One of the reasons we're discussing this use of the term here is that it is a trap for the unwary, and can become a club in the hands of the jealous.

While my intent is to resist making pronouncements, I am under no compulsion to obscure or confuse. With each of these terms we encounter the same kind of invention (like Hume's virtuous horse)—a solid, huggable word—to signify the existence of something that interests us. The invention serves an essential purpose not only in our conversations but in our thinking. We can move it around as chess players move knights and bishops, trying to capture the king, or the way mathematicians move x's and y's in their equations, trying to trap an elusive number. X is the unknown in an equation ($x = 27 - y$). Timbre, melody, and *tone* are also unknowns, but we forget that.

Each of these words, it seems to me, represents an attempt to bridge the distance between concepts in physiology, mechanics, and physics on the one hand and related concepts in aesthetics on the other. Our interest in them is not abstract; as we explore their genesis and use, we find it impossible to make sense of anything unless we grant the validity of the following proposition: The roles of musician and listener are remarkably active and similar, at least insofar as the auditory system is concerned. The same is likely to be true of the aesthetics of the musical experience. Neither the musician's nor the listener's contribution is passive, no matter how relaxed and comfortable the job may seem. We will look at these terms, therefore, in the hope that they will give us greater insight into the happy and mysterious interaction we call music.

Timbre, like pitch, is a judgment which results from the acoustic output of an object (wastebasket, piano, oboe, or your Uncle Irving) reaching an ear that is wired to an attentive brain. Whereas the pitch of a note has to do with its fidelity to the choreography of a melodic dance, timbre has more to do with the personality or individuality displayed in the execution of the steps. Part of that personality is attributable to the instrument producing the tone. Specifically, timbre is most often regarded as an aspect of sound quality due to the physical makeup of the instrument.

Musical instruments, as duly noted elsewhere, have been with us for at least as long as the recorded history of civilization. They evolved through experimentation (without government grants), doubtless under the influence of a sort of Darwinian evolutionary force favoring survival of the fittest. Instruments that worked, could be reliably controlled, and pleased the musicians and listeners tended to be reproduced and to proliferate. Our musical affections being what they are, instrumental manufacture has by now reached a high level of refinement. The acoustical benefits are important; oboes sound like oboes, trumpets like trumpets, and so on.

But what exactly does that mean? How do we, in the audience, tell the clarinet from the flute, or the trumpet from the violin (especially when they are playing tones of the same pitch)? What about different instruments of the same type—can we really tell one violin from another, or hear a difference in an oboe or a French horn when its owner changes reed or mouthpiece? If so, how do we manage it?

In the most general terms, the answer seems to be something like this. With the exception of electronic instruments, no instrument ever generates a pure tone—a tone of a single frequency. Because of its structure, and the way sound is coaxed out of it, every musical instrument produces a characteristic mix of frequencies when it is played. It is mainly the size of the instrument, the thickness of its walls, the shape of its resonant structures, and the location and character of the frequency generator which determine the character and behavior of individual and blended frequencies which can be produced.

The construction of the instrument affects listener judgments about it in a variety of ways. First, largely independent of the player's intent to control volume, sounds produced by each instrument rise and fall in intensity in a way determined by the mechanics of the sound-generating mechanism. Instruments that are bowed, for example, cannot generate a sharp or staccato sound as easily (or convincingly) as can a percussion instrument. The difference between tones produced by cellos and xylophones, in this sense, invites comparison with the behavior of motorcyles and school buses at a traffic light that has just turned green.

Auditory engineers have developed a device able to show how long it takes for a tone of any frequency to reach maximum intensity. The change of amplitude of any frequency as the tone is played is called its envelope, and the envelope of the fundamental frequency (the one which gives rise to the harmonics) seems to hold the secret to our ability to identify specific instruments. It's all in the getaway—the length of time it takes the fundamental to get to maximum intensity tells us what we're listening to.

The second important auditory consequence of the design of the instrument has to do with the way it develops and blends its family of overtones. Although the harmonic series is mathematically derived, neither clarinets nor French horns (nor anything else, for that matter) follow the rules exactly, or deviate from the rules in quite the same way. Pianos (which can be precisely tuned) are not even *allowed* to follow the rules exactly. Those eons of trial and error begat a profusion of scientifically ragged but musically sublime noisemakers, because the arbiter in this struggle for survival has been not the oscilloscope but the ear.

After the getaway, the tone settles down and its component frequencies get more comfortable with one another. At this point, the mix of frequencies tells the listener two things: first, that the same instrument that started the tone is still producing it; second, that the tone is comprised of a series of harmonics belonging to a specific pitch family. In midtone, for example, the frequency mix (timbre) confirms that you're still listening to the oboe, and it's playing an F or thereabouts.

None of this could happen were it not for the sound detection and analysis system at your disposal when the curtain goes up. Despite the enormous complexity and speed of change of all these component frequencies, the auditory system is well equipped to discern who's doing what. Every instrument (electronic instruments are the exception, sometimes) generates tones which in physiologic terms are extremely long in duration. Even a staccato tone evolves and can be studied by the auditory system at a snail's pace in comparison to the pace of events in the nervous system. The pianist's hand may be quicker than the eye, but the tones he plays are not quicker than the ear.*

Timbre, as we shall see, is a product of both the design of the instrument and the technique of the musician. Later we shall consider what this means in relationship to musical *tone.* This will be like returning to the metaphor of the school bus and the motorcycle to inquire whether things would be different if I were driving the motorcycle and Mario Andretti were in charge of the school bus.

The great complexity and subtlety of this aspect of musical experience has begun to be appreciated recently by two modern entrants into the musical world. I refer to the designers of electronic instruments (synthesizers) and the composers of electronic music. What they have discovered, among other things, is that it is very tough to get an electronic instrument to sound like a "real" instrument. Since the designer seeks to achieve sounds which the ear will judge to be familiar, he must have at least two classes of information: First, he must know precisely the

*If you care to explore this somewhat treacherous field in a way intended for musicians, read the excellent text on acoustics by Dr. Arthur Benade, a physicist who is himself an accomplished clarinetist.[1] Or, with less risk to the ego, you can read the charming review of his personal experiences by the pianist Gary Graffman.[2]

acoustic characteristics of any instrument he wishes to imitate; second, he must have a code enabling the translation of these specifications into instructions to his sound generator to behave acoustically in the desired way.

Listening to synthesizers has convinced many people that the engineers are skillful in the creation of new effects, some of which are quite musical and appealing. However, mimicking the sounds of other instruments has proven more taxing than anyone expected. The sounds of the organ, harpsichord, guitar, and drum have proven relatively simple to analyze and re-create; other instrumental sounds are not so easily formulated.*

The search for an explanation of this difficulty in music synthesis has recently taken an unexpected turn. Although much is known about the acoustic performance of specific instruments, and there is no practical limit to the capabilities of the electronic devices used to produce sound, it had not been suspected that the *listener* might prove to be the nemesis of the electronic wizards. In truth, there is nothing lacking in the capabilities of the computers and sound generators. The problem has to do with the near impossibility of cracking the code used by the auditory system to process sound information.

There is, in other words, another class of information that may be required for the synthesis of musical sounds if experienced listeners are to judge them to be authentic. This has to do with the way the human auditory system processes and analyzes sounds presented to it.

Milton Babbitt, who not only was the most influential pioneer

---

*The nightmarish magnitude and subtlety of this problem is immediately apparent from the observations of musicians who complain of the "enormous difference" between the sound of two pianos, or two oboes, made in the same factory by the same craftsmen, using closely matched materials. For a superb account of the problem from the piano builder's point of view, see Michael Lenehan's piece in the *Atlantic Monthly*.[3]

in American electronic music composition but remains a dominant force at its frontier, has put the matter in straightforward and succinct terms: "What can this machine do? What can this performer do? The new limitations are the most mysterious and little understood of limitations: what can be heard?"[4]

It is important to understand what Mr. Babbitt is saying. Until now, it was possible to say that some folks have good ears, and some just don't. Now all bets are off; the speed and brevity with which computers and synthesizers can generate sounds has forced a revolution in thinking about the perception of music. It is now necessary to talk about physiology, because composers can write, and synthesizers can play, music that exceeds the detection and analytic capabilities of even the most sophisticated ear. Moreover, a new curve has been thrown: The scientists who study human auditory perception tell us that the popular "left brain–right brain" dichotomy is hopelessly oversimplified. At least insofar as the job of detecting and processing auditory information is concerned, no two ears, and no two brains, ever do this job in the same way. However convoluted the problem becomes, this much is clear: No longer is it possible to take the listener (or listening) for granted.

The problem of what can be heard has always been at the heart of the musical experience. This is true in the most diverse circumstances: an audience listening to a single instrument, a symphony with full chorus, or a synthesizer; the musician rehearsing alone or with others in an ensemble, playing in front of or behind the curtain; a conductor imagining the sound of his orchestra as he sits in his study examining a new musical score, then hearing it from the podium during a concert. It is true of you whenever and wherever you play an instrument or sing, no matter what the stage of your musical development.

We are now obliged, however, to consider the listening experience in a new light. We no longer have much trouble accepting the notion that playing skills, and artistry, require the refinement of physiologic potential. Now, though, it appears that our responsiveness as listeners is the other side of the same coin, in ways that tend to confirm and might extend the implications of Mr. Copland's aforementioned opinions about music appreciation.

At first reading, we can draw from the newest research a sense that we are close to having scientific validation of the precept that there are benefits awaiting anyone willing to cultivate his or her own musical sensitivity; certainly, there is no doubt auditory perception will be shown to be compatible with, and doubtless to share, biologic operations common to other physiologic systems known to have the capacity to improve their operating efficiency ("Practice makes perfect!"). But in honesty we must acknowledge that we still lack what the legal profession likes to call the smoking gun: We can't prove that any specific aspect of listening skill improved because of an event in the life of the listener. It remains to be shown scientifically that "learning how to listen" involves changing the way the brain works.

As much as you might pine for this consummation of art and science, I think you had best heed a warning. If it *can* be shown that we can hear only what we've learned how to hear, and that no two listeners can ever be biologically the same, some of our most treasured notions about aesthetics are in for heavy weather. We'll get to that problem in just a bit, after we dispense with one of the things you *try* to listen for.

If you have a terrific memory, you will recall that we have one piece of unfinished business from the guitar concert. This concerns the feeling we might have had during the piece that we'd heard a wrong note. To keep things simple, let us say we heard a tone that was not part of, and therefore disrupted the continuity of, the melody.

What this means physiologically (or psychologically) is that somehow we knew in advance the intended order of the notes and heard a tone, or tones, out of the expected order. This could have happened even though we had never heard the music before. How? In order to understand the question (I'll tell you now that I can't give you an answer), we need to take a closer look at the word *melody*.

In one sense, the idea of a melody is straightforward: Each note in the piece defines an intended pitch, and as the piece moves rhythmically from start to finish, the variations in pitch of its tones create a contour, or musical line, meant to be perceived by the listener as the unifying idea of the piece. If I ask you to think of "Yankee Doodle Dandy," and you are familiar with the piece, you will recall a timed pattern of musical pitches in a sequence most of us would agree "belongs to" "Yankee Doodle Dandy." That is its melody.

To say more than this requires great courage and imagination. In truth, we are venturing into very deep water here: Contemporary theorists of musical structure lean heavily on the concepts and terminolgy of linguistics, and you may find yourself doing a lot of deep breathing if you try to read what they have to say about structural principles in music, or the basis of musical meaning. It is not at all certain that visitors are welcome to the inner sanctum. Leonard Bernstein tried to gain entry a few years back, and was treated like a party-crasher.*

In most cases you will look in vain on a musical score for arrows or colors or other messages to indicate that "these notes make up the melody." Yet we hear a stream of tones, one after

*For the devotee of curious intellectual dialogues, one could hardly find a more interesting example than this. Bernstein, intrigued with the remarkable work of Noam Chomsky (particularly the idea of a universal grammar), postulated an analogous mechanism to explain the consistency of human responsiveness to musical form and discussed his ideas in a series of lectures given at Harvard in 1973.[5] This contribution earned mixed reviews, ultimately being ruled naive by the "experts."[6]

another, and we link or unify them into a perceptual bunch (or category) which we call the melody. The melody itself is only one of the currents in what is often a broadly flowing stream of sound, full of right tones. What is a wrong note? You see what the difficulty is: Who decides what the *right* note is? Is it the composer? If so, how does he tell us? We are dealing here with a genuine mystery. It has to do with something that happens spontaneously (an auditory hallucination?) in the internal auditory space of a composer, which he tries to re-create for us, his listeners, through his music.

Perhaps melody should be spelled *melodie* and sit at the top of the list of French words not ready to be translated into English. Melody is what's left in a single-file progression of pitches when you've stripped everything else away. Melody is what you hum or whistle when someone asks you, "How does 'Home on the Range' go?"

This issue is well beyond the scope of this book. However, it is not one you should ignore. If you are interested, your curiosity and tenacity will be greatly rewarded by reviewing this subject in detail in Diana Deutsch's book, *The Psychology of Music.*[7]

We are now ready to wrestle with the real dragon, musical *tone.* Earlier, we considered the means by which we distinguish between different instruments when they play. What we must approach next is the basis of judgments we make about the identity and skill of the musician playing the instrument (or singing). Of course, we're not talking about the differences between Heifetz and your Uncle Irving on the violin—that's an interesting problem to address but not so interesting as this: Can blindfolded listeners discern that not one but two pianists have played the same music on the same instrument, when each is following the score accurately?

To avert the valid objection that differences in interpretation would make the truth obvious, the experimental question could be posed like this: Might two pianists playing the same music on the same piano lead you to believe you are listening to the same artist playing two different instruments? Or, can a violinist playing the same music on a cheap violin and an expensive violin cause you to believe the same instrument is being played twice? You may suspect we're getting into an ivory tower aspect of music here, and I wouldn't disagree. However, this is precisely where careers are made and lost in the big leagues. Why?

It used to be hotly argued that the touch of a pianist could not influence sound produced by the piano apart from controlling the speed of succession of notes (by varying the interval between finger depressions) or their volume (by varying the speed of attack of each note). Hence, as Sir James Jeans asserted, one could produce the same *tone* with an umbrella tip as with a fingertip.[8]

I am told that each of the experiments described beginning two paragraphs ago has been carried out, and that the results are unequivocal. In all of these cases the performer can influence the behavior of the instrument so that the perceptual illusions described do occur. It is precisely as with Mario at the wheel of the bus versus me at the controls of the motorcycle. There is not the slightest doubt that observers would be able to tell who was driving what.

Yet the argument about *tone* goes on, in relation to the skills of particular artists. As with that elusive commodity talent, *tone* is something one either has or doesn't have, and is recognized as a personal signature of an artist just as timbre is recognized as the personal signature of an instrument. I think the claims about particular musicians would have a less deterministic and global flavor if they took greater account of the small details of dynamic and rhythmic execution—interpretation, if you will —achieved in the performance of specific music.

The ongoing blend and continuity of musical sound give rise to an interdependent set of perceptual judgments in the listener, and in any given piece of music the illusory effect ("this reminds me of that gorgeous meadow in Wisconsin") may turn on that fraction of a second of overtime put in by an E preceding a G#. The artist's interpretation of music, after all, is realized only through the sounds made by the instrument. If we had a clearer objective picture of how a successful artist assembles sounds as he or she makes music of them, the rest of us might aspire to having a beautiful *tone*, too.

This brings us to the last and by every criterion I can think of the most interesting form of the questions about *tone*: Can the same artist in a single performance make two listeners believe they are listening to two different performances? As you know, from the reviews quoted in the first of these chapters on auditory perception, the answer is yes.

And so, we have come full circle. It is as Mr. Babbitt said: The problem is, what can be heard? But it is not simply a matter of the physiologic limits of the cochlea and auditory cortex. It is also a matter of the idiosyncrasies of individual listeners. We may have gone beyond the philosopher's question: Do two music critics, or other listeners, sometimes hear different performances? We may have to confront the physiologist's question: Can two individuals ever hear the *same* performance?

It was not long after I had made the personal discovery that I could hear too much pedal in a Mozart recording that I decided to find out something about this unexpected change in my own ability to discern small musical details. I had been musing over this for a few months when I happened to see the notice of a lecture to be given at a medical center not far from my own office. The lecture, "Mechanisms in Central Auditory Processing," was being given by Dr. Robert Efron, a man with the reputation of being a neurophysiologist's neurophysiologist. That means he knows as much about brain function as anyone is entitled to know.

I went to the lecture, given in a small conference room in the hospital, crowded with residents and graduate students who were eagerly devouring the talk and their lunches at the same time. I listened carefully, took notes, went back to my office, and moped for a few days. The talk had been a technical review of a special investigative procedure called "dichotic listening" and I had understood very little of it.

Several weeks later I decided to swallow my wounded pride. I had to confess my ignorance and get on with my education. So I called Dr. Efron, introduced myself, and asked to visit him. He agreed and we met shortly thereafter. I explained my interest in brain mechanisms in music (until then I had concentrated my attention on the motor control system). I told him I had been coming around to the idea that hearing had a great deal to do with refinement of motor control, and it was my wish to learn more about the interaction of these two physiologic systems. As a preliminary, clearly, I would have to abandon my eighteenth-century ideas about human auditory perception.

We have since become very good friends, but at that moment I felt extremely insecure as he silently contemplated the oddball (me) sitting on the other side of his desk. After some thought he told me that it was something of a coincidence that I had sought him out. He had been doing research in human auditory perception for some years, and (as he jokingly put it) "you couldn't find a bigger ignoramus about music than me." However, he added, he had recently come to the conclusion that there must be something extraordinary about the hearing of musicians. He had reached a point in his work that seemed to call for comparative studies of perceptual ability in musicians and nonmusicians. We struck a bargain: He would try to teach me something about human hearing, and I would try to round up some musicians for his lab.

Dr. Efron, an early member of the growing community of

physiologists concerned with human perception, has made a number of highly original contributions to our understanding of both visual and auditory processing.[9] One of his many interests has to do with spatially localized cognitive processes. However complex this may sound (and in fact certainly is, neurologically), it is a familiar part of your everyday experience. If you will pay close attention the next time you listen to a good stereo recording of familiar music, you will be aware that you can follow independently almost any audible instrument in the recording. You will find the same thing true at a concert. You can close your eyes and follow a single instrument, almost as though it were the solo instrument, even though others around it are playing at higher volume. You may be able to follow the sound of more than one instrument at a time.

Think about this for a moment: Because of your remarkable auditory ability, you can hear a musical group in stereo. Because of your ability to detect, analyze, and compare any number of exquisitely small details of individual tones, you can identify specific instruments in the ensemble. Add to this the ability to shift your attention at will through the sounds and track anything of interest, and you begin to appreciate the remarkable degree of control you routinely exercise over your own auditory input. You can and *do* hear what you listen for.

The most recent work in Dr. Efron's laboratory suggests that our selective spatial attention and discrimination depend on reverse direction messages going from the brain to the ears. It has long been known that such a pathway exists in the brain, but it has not been known what its purpose is, or how it operates. It has been suspected that such a system could modify the sensitivity of the cochlea of stimuli reaching it, or modify its own processing of those stimuli. The newest work suggests that the system not only is capable of such influence but in all likelihood is the determining factor in our ability to locate meaningful sounds and to pay attention to those of greatest interest. What musicians call ear training almost certainly involves this sort of active, searching listening, which could scarcely take place without an internal model of what is being looked for. The work that goes into building internal models must change the functional capacity of the system, but (as noted earlier) we lack proof and haven't the slightest idea how it would work in any case.

It might appear that our consideration of the auditory system is moving from the sublime to the ridiculous in its final stages, but I would like to conclude by inviting you to reflect on the differences between you and my adorable cat, or any other creature you might prefer to think about. In particular, I would like you to consider the following question: Why isn't my cat interested in opera, or folk music, or rock 'n' roll? I used to think she should be. She has superb hearing acuity, and the same mechanisms for pitch discrimination you and I have. I know she can identify other animals by their sounds, since she cowers inside the house when a particularly unpleasant bluejay is in the neighborhood. Her vocalizing is rudimentary, but even with a vocabulary limited to a few distinctive meows she manages to get me to do most of the tricks she's taught me. She, and some of her acquaintances, sing from time to time.

Her piano playing never seems to improve. Despite the long hours she puts in at the keyboard (normally between 4 and 5 in the morning), I never expect to hear her play Scarlatti's G Minor Sonata (The Cat's Fugue).

Other living things make and respond to noise in quite elaborate ways. Crickets and frogs give concerts, bats use their voices and hearing to navigate and chase down prey. I was recently introduced to a parrot who not only vocalizes the way parrots are supposed to but also sings along with her owner well enough to perform onstage with him. She sings a few popular songs, carries a tune quite well, and doesn't get the lyrics mixed up. I don't know if she has ever been to an opera. As we look at other mammals with brains not unlike ours, we encounter vocalizing so poignant and artful (as with the use of sign language by certain apes) that it might be best to restrain our pride; we may one day have to relinquish our putative sole claim to true musicality. Time will tell.

There is no serious argument that other animals communicate with sound (including the expression of emotion), or that they have the capacity to respond to sound in precisely the "sensuous" way Copland described in his comments on the ways we listen to music. What is so different about *human* responsiveness to and use of musical sound?

Since I am not qualified to give anything like an authoritative opinion on this question, I feel at liberty to guess. A broadly conceived answer, I suspect, would refer to the construction of both the auditory and muscular systems, and to their connections with the rest of the brain. What we do musically that is special, compared to other living things, comes down to the possession of a broad and malleable appetite, fascination with variety and subtlety, and the ability to modify our own skills as we search for new ways to organize, display, and employ sound.

Ethnomusicologists, the historians who study existing musical instruments in human culture and musical artifacts, tell us that the earliest instruments were attached to the body so as to embellish its rhythmic movement. Somehow it must have been found that pitch as well as rhythm could be controlled by manipulation of sound-producing objects. This would require in most instances the use of the hands (sometimes with lips and mouth) to turn these objects into tools. Thus having acquired the ability to imitate pitch changes of the human voice, or of other natural sounds, our music-making ancestors were in business.

Some of our musical practices could easily have developed from the coincident possession of mammalian auditory skills and those required to build and use tools. But possession of the tools would have meant little without a muscular control system allowing progressive refinement in control of arm, hand, and orofacial movement, and the possibility of guidance of such movement by the sounds elicited from the instruments. This is a subject we have already considered in some detail.

Contact by the auditory and muscular control systems with the integrated neurologic systems responsible for linguistic, computational, and visual-spatial competence (as well as those involved in emotional behavior) permits music to participate in and to influence virtually all of the other general operations of the human central nervous system. In the final analysis, the open-endedness and adaptability of human behavior (including musical behavior), and what we refer to as creativity, must flow from these elements and their contact with one another. Lacking this arrangement, my cat and the singing parrot would at the very most regard Bach, Beethoven, Brubeck, Babbitt, or the Beatles as a pleasant aroma for the ears.

Lastly, lacking the words to say so, it would not occur to them to observe that music (as with other forms of art) allows us to explore our individuality and our universality, our mortality and our immortality, all at once.

As we think about our own musicality, in contrast to that of other members of the animal kingdom, we can feel overwhelmed by the complexity of the facts and fine details, or reassured by the ultimate simplicity of the truth. We need not be scared off—music is not just for the people in conservatories. There's no right way to play (since no two people can possibly produce the same sound), and there's no right way to listen—since no one else will ever be able to hear music as we hear it. So we don't need to feel foolish about conducting this highly personal expedition in our own way. If someone else wants to listen to what we do, that's *their* problem.

Notes

1. Arthur Benade, *Fundamentals of Musical Acoustics*, Oxford University Press, 1976.
2. Gary Graffman, "Pianist in the Basement" (Chapter 11), in *I Really Should Be Practicing*, Doubleday, 1981.
3. Michael Lenehan, "The Quality of the Instrument," *Atlantic Monthly*, August 1982, pp. 32–58.
4. Quoted in Robert Commanday, "Biology of Music Making," *San Francisco Chronicle* (review), September 30, 1984, pp. 14–15.
5. Leonard Bernstein, *The Unanswered Question: Six Talks at Harvard* (The Charles Eliot Norton Lectures, 1973), Harvard University Press, 1976.
6. Ray Jackendoff and Fred Lerdahl, "A Grammatical Parallel Between Music and Language," in *Music, Mind and Brain*, ed. Manfred Clynes, Plenum Press, 1982.
7. Diana Deutsch, "Grouping Mechanisms in Music," in *The Psychology of Music*, ed. Diana Deutsch, Academic Press (Series in Cognition and Perception), 1982, pp. 99–135.
8. Donal Henahan, "Of Piano Tone and Umbrella Tips," *The New York Times*, February 28, 1982, Section 2, p. 2.
9. Robert Efron, "Experimental Psychoacoustics of the Central Auditory System: Five Myths," in *Assessment of Central Auditory Dysfunction: Its Foundations and Clinical Correlates*, eds. M. Pinheiro and F. Musiek, Academic Press. In Press.

8

Time in Your Hands

GETTING FROM HERE TO THERE IN AN ORDERLY FASHION

During the many years of their close friendship, Albert Schweitzer and Albert Einstein often played chamber music together. The story of one such session, if it is to be believed, reveals these two extraordinary men in a way that will comfort those of us who must make our way through life as mere mortals.

Einstein, the mathematician and theoretical physicist, was having a rough time with a rhythmically difficult passage. Schweitzer, the missionary and Nobel Peace Prize winner, was having an equally rough time with his temper. Finally, after several unsuccessful attempts to influence the Einstein rendering of the music, Schweitzer gave in to his exasperation: "Count! Count! *Dammit,* Albert, can't you count?"

For some people, just *walking* in a rhythmic way seems almost too much to hope for. I recall from my years in a high school marching band, as a snare drummer, that most kids could pick up the feel of a marching cadence quickly, while a few seemed impervious to the concept that people walking or marching together could move legs and feet in unison. The folklore of marching organizations is rich with references to the occasional hapless marcher whose shoes had to be labeled Left and Right so that he could decide how to respond to the spoken commands of the drum major. Those of us who did not suffer this disability tended to be impatient, mostly, I think, because we felt you either had it (the ability to keep in step) or you didn't. The kids who didn't have it were wasting their time and ours, and they were not encouraged to remain. Such is the tyranny of ignorance and conformity!

A few years ago I was intrigued to watch an exercise now popular with marching bands called a drill down. I suppose the Marines invented it. In this exercise, the drum major conducts a contest using a series of marching commands, the object being to confuse and trip up the marchers, eliminate those who make mistakes, and thereby discover the kid with ears on his ankles. The exercise convinced me that marching must follow the same basic rules that apply to virtually every other motor skill. Some learn faster than others, experience counts, and everyone has limits.

In the earlier chapters on auditory and motor system physiology, our search for clues to human musicianship had a double payoff. Not only did we find evidence of rich and varied operation of these systems in nonmusical tasks, we concluded that their employment for music just meant mixing and stretching potential we all possess but tend to keep on the shelf. We now turn our attention to the matter of timing, an early and continuing aspect of musical competence. What is known about the physiologic basis of this ability, and what does it have to do with musicianship?

At the outset, it should be noted that we probably do not possess a timing system that is anatomically distinct, in the sense that the auditory and motor systems are. All we can say now is that a number of physiologic processes take place in ways that are time-dependent, running their course on a scale that ranges from milliseconds to months. The undisputed temporal orderliness of these processes does not necessarily signify the presence of a single timing system in the body; we may be looking at an attribute of a number of systems. This is like moving from the study of combustion systems in cars to a consideration of heat dispersion. There is no guarantee we will find a radiator under the hood.

Nevertheless we shall look, and for good reason. Once again we will find evidence of highly developed ability in us all, with ample room for growth. This is true no matter what others might think of our potential as members of a drill team, or of any specific experiences along those lines we might have had. More exciting, though, is the possibility that we will be able to gain insight into an aspect of musical experience which has long been taken for granted, but which is beginning to emerge as one of its greatest mysteries—I am referring to musical time, tempo, and rhythm. Newer ideas about the physiology of timing suggest to some people that the related musical concepts are due for a fresh look.

I have always had what I thought a curious mixture of natural rhythm together with a sense that I was on thin ice when trying to translate the rhythmic pattern of notes on a page into a succession of notes accurately executed in time. It is easy enough to say that this is a reading problem, which it may well be, but I think there's more to it.

I think it has to do with the yin and yang of tempo and rhythm, two basic elements of a system which governs the timing of melody and harmony in music as it proceeds from beginning to end.

As we shall see, the postulate of dual timing mechanisms in music fits quite well with emerging ideas regarding control of the timing of bodily functions. It wouldn't be a bad idea to hedge our bets and grant the existence of *at least* two kinds of timing in music—nothing is ever as simple as one supposes.

Let's take tempo first. Tempo refers to the *pace* at which music evolves. It is the reference system that ties music to the ebb and flow of our own physical processes. The composer sets the length of time between separate beats in a musical piece so that we can begin to make our connections with it. When the music is played, we normally respond immediately to its tempo with specific expectations—this music is going to make us dance, march, or snooze, or it may make us want to laugh, or cry.

And what is rhythm? In its most fundamental sense, rhythm is the patterning of events that take place *between* successive beats. However long the interval between beats may be, it can be subdivided into smaller units of time. The choices the composer makes about breaking up these intervals are choices that determine the rhythm.

It is not hard to see why we tend to regard rhythm and tempo as part of a unified element of music. Both can be represented by simple physical movements which mark the passage of time. Dancing feet, clapping hands, and flying drumsticks produce sounds which describe tempo and rhythm simultaneously; some of the notes in written music do the same double duty. The bodily movements which execute music's tempo and rhythm are so smoothly coordinated that there is good reason to suspect that they operate jointly under the influence of a stable timing device—a clock. If so, where is the clock located? And how does it work?

As musicians, we are inclined to be both romantic and bemused in our attitudes about tempo, rhythm, and the clock. Our instincts impel us to *feel* the beat of the music (or to follow the prompting of our hearts, both literally and figuratively). Despite our somewhat mysticophysiologic leanings, we are pragmatists accustomed to the dictates of composers, metronomes, and conductors. Hence we may find the idea of an internal clock interesting but irrelevant. Often enough we are advised to set our feelings aside and follow instructions, are we not? Perhaps so, but the question is not so easily subdued. Where does our internal sense of tempo really come from, and how reliable is it?

Is it thrown off when we're nervous, or have had too much coffee? When someone else sets the beat, how do we manage to follow it?

It would seem that there are both theoretical and practical reasons for musicians to concern themselves with the biology of timing, and to acquaint themselves with some of the work that has already been done by students of this fascinating aspect of our makeup.

Psychologists and physiologists have been interested in this issue for a number of years, mainly because of the occurrence of a variety of cycles and other timed events in our lives. You are already well acquainted with most of these: We sleep about the same amount, and at about the same time, every day; we get hungry and eat on schedule; female ovulation resembles the cycle of the lunar month.

Then, of course, there is the matter of our heartbeat and our breathing. These two cycles at the very core of life are now a familiar bridge between the vocabularies of musicians and biologists. It seems sensible to me that we begin our small scientific excursion by reflecting on this intriguing coincidence.

Our bodies require a steady supply of oxygen—without it we are done for in just a few minutes. Consequently, we pay attention to our breathing and our pulse. Our concern for these fundamental cyclic bodily processes sensitizes us to the movement of our own bodies, and seems to kindle a peculiar sensitivity to *outside* events whose rhythmicity suggests our own.

We are attentive not only to the presence of rhythms that pulse and breathe but also to even slight variations in their tempo. Just as roller skaters and skiers feel the rise and fall of any terrain on which they move, we can detect immediately the slightest increase in our own pulse and breathing.

Rhythmic or pulsed movement has significant hypnotic potential. Indeed, music often takes advantage of this tendency.

It is likely you have already experienced at least a light trance while listening to music, and it may happen to you regularly. It can happen with any kind of music, including rock 'n' roll. Since people often report being especially refreshed after being in a trance, this may explain some music's legendary power to heal and to revitalize.

If you have never to your knowledge been in trance, a word of explanation may be in order. During a normal waking state, our attention shifts according to immediate goals and whatever intrusions the environment presents. We concentrate on whatever is of the greatest importance or interest, with a peripheral awareness which is not focused but is nevertheless prepared to respond to random surprises. If we happen to be doing something which demands attention but which is habitual, our thoughts tend to drift. Thus, when we drive we are prone to daydreaming, and may briefly become entirely oblivious of our surroundings. Luckily, we do this most often when waiting at stoplights, where the main hazard is the primitive aggression of the driver behind us whose urgent trip to the beach we have delayed by responding sluggishly to the green light.

The next time you are on a quiet evening walk, or mindlessly gnawing on a bone, pay attention to your own subjective feelings and to your sense of the passage of time. The pleasant haze in which the irritations of the world are obscured, and in which time passes without notice, is a trance. As with music, you may have fallen effortlessly into this state under the influence of repetitious movement.

You may sense that we have come upon another bridge. The heart and lungs, it seems, have the capacity to reach into the brain not only with blood and oxygen but with the feel of their own movement. Is it possible that music travels on this physiologic pathway? We are getting very close to poetry here (which shouldn't disturb your musical instincts), but we haven't left the company of the scientists quite yet. There *is* a way to look at rhythmic activity in the brain. It's done with a machine called an electroencephalograph. Let's cross the second bridge.

It has been something like fifty years since the first electrical recordings of brain activity were obtained. The ability to do this has been a boon to physicians, and others, eager to understand more about both normal and disordered function in the brain. As it is usually carried out, the test involves applying to the scalp small electrodes connected to a recording machine. As the patient relaxes, a tracing can be made of minute fluctuations in electrical charge at the brain's surface. Most often the pattern of activity observed is random, but there are times when it becomes rhythmic, either in specific regions of the brain or over its entire surface. When the electrical signals are rhythmic, they are felt to reflect pulsed charges involving widely dispersed networks of brain cells.

Among the brain wave patterns observed with this technique, that seen most commonly over the back of the head has perhaps attracted the most interest (much of which comes from outside the medical community). Called alpha waves, these occur at a frequency between eight and twelve times each second. They are of special interest because of an unexplained relationship between prominent alpha wave activity in the brain and the subjective feeling of relaxation. As yet, though, alpha waves have *not* been shown to have a specific relationship to trance, or to music. Nor has any other complex form of behavior been linked to brain waves of a particular form found here, there, or somewhere else. So far, the electronic version of phrenologic frenzy remains largely unrewarded.

We may have come to a point where science fades and mysticism begins. But we have not really exhausted the supply of bridges between music and physiology—breathing and heartbeat are not the only rhythmic movements we should consider.

The full list of timed physiologic events includes both automatic internal processes and a variety of physical movements over which we have voluntary control. Walking and chewing are the basic movements of mobility and nutrition, and as such are essential to our survival as individuals. These movements are learned early in life, and tend to be stereotyped, automatic, and evenly paced. The idea of walking as a reference for musical tempo is conveyed by the Italian term *andante.*

The survival of the species is dependent on procreation, and we meet our obligations to the genetic trust with a repertoire of movements which can range from the simple to the exotic, but which invariably display (at some point in their unfolding) the familiar and important signature of inherent rhythmicity. So far as I know, neither the Italians nor anyone else has a term to refer to the tempo suggested by this sort of activity.

All of these maintenance activities can evoke the emotions, and at times do so with great intensity. The feelings generated by the discovery of a rapid pulse at the wrist of a favorite companion are dramatic, though not so dramatic as those reported to accompany the discovery of an absent pulse at one's own wrist. People have even been known to swoon at the prospect of chewing on a chocolate bar.

In sum, on the matter of pulse, breathing, munching, and so on, we are entitled to say something like the following: Much of our ongoing life is involved in automatic or nearly automatic processes which are cyclic and rhythmic. We are not often attentive to these on a minute-by-minute basis, but our subjective feelings of comfort and discomfort are strongly conditioned by the operation (including the rhythmic pace) of all this machinery. Moreover, our emotions are easily aroused when there is a need for us to step in on a conscious level to bring one of the physiologic systems back to a state of equilibrium. The temptation is great to link certain electrical rhythms in the brain to bodily rhythms, and to arousal and the emotions, but the nature and relative influence of these relationships is still a matter of speculation.

Musicians, and musical theorists, have not been blind to all this pulsing, sighing, and throbbing in our lives, and have cited the parallels between musical and bodily rhythms to explain the universal appeal of music in human culture. Tempo is not simply a device employed mechanically to reckon movement in a piece from beginning to end. When it is conveyed through beats or pulses which imitate the body's timed or cyclic processes, it seems able to influence us in specific and dramatic ways. It is as though music had the capacity to plug the brain into itself briefly in a novel way, by linking rhythmic muscular activity to brain mechanisms in control of alertness, attention, and emotion. So there really isn't such a mystery after all. Music accompanies, imitates, and in some cases improves on that which the body is already doing. It's a beautiful system, and it all fits.

The trouble with this explanation is that it is too true to be good. It makes pulse not only dominant but distinctly domineering in our thinking; there is simply too much left unexplained, and we are obliged to acknowledge the deficiencies. I propose now to explain my suspicion that our theories on the power of music suffer somewhat in the soothing but monotonous embrace of circulatory and respiratory physiology.

All musical tones, as we have seen, have a fundamental frequency, overtones, and elements called formants which help us identify their source. They also have, at least theoretically, a duration. It is by specifying the duration of the individual notes that the composer divides up the time at his disposal between beats. He can fill up this time any way he likes, but cannot ignore it. This is where the problems, and the prospects for discovery, begin—this lands the composer, the musician, and us (breathless and near cardiac arrest) in the scientist's world of mathematics and psychophysics, where tempo and rhythm demand separate consideration.

In the good old days, before people wrote music down, there was no problem. You watched people move their feet and clap their hands, listened to the drums, gourds, whistles, flutes, or fiddles, and before you knew it you were ready to jump in and add to the fun. You could invent variations on someone else's patterns and ornaments, slide around the beat, syncopate, generally go crazy, and nobody would ever know you couldn't read a dotted eighth note followed by a sixteenth if your life depended on it. Unfortunately, written music is like double-entry bookkeeping when it represents the timing of events. Only it's the end of the measure rather than the end of the month when everything has to balance—the total span of time consumed by all the events in a measure cannot exceed the duration of that measure.

This brings us back to the clock, only from the point of view of the motor system: How do we manage to time the onset and duration of skilled movements, and fit them into the tempo scheme of the music? After looking at a musical score as a sort of mathematical code, we need only glance briefly at drummers, flutists, violinists, or pianists (singly and in groups) to see that they are doing far more than simply clapping their hands to keep a beat. We need something beyond our celebrated sensitivity to pulse to account for the striking refinement and complexity of the timing skills observed in accomplished musical execution.

We have already considered the built-in rhythmicity of the heart and lungs, and toyed a bit with theories as to how the brain could be influenced by pulse and breathing. What we must now consider is what the brain uses as a reference in the regulation of the timing of movement in the muscles under its control. This was a matter alluded to, but not explored, in the earlier chapters on the motor system.

There are at least two ways we might prove the existence of a bona fide internal clock capable of controlling the timing of voluntary movements. We might do so by comparing personal estimates of time to that marked by a real clock; if it could be shown that people can accurately and consistently report the passage of discrete time intervals on their own, one would have to suppose that we have some internal equivalent of a Swiss watch ticking away inside to keep us on schedule. The examples of such skill that can be cited are few and rather modest: Some of us get up in the morning a minute or so before the alarm goes off; the doctor feels your pulse for a few seconds, doesn't look at the clock, and pronounces your heart rate a gratifying 68 beats per minute.

What about musicians? There is no dispute about the rhythmic accuracy displayed by the seasoned performer who is playing music that has been well rehearsed. If this skill were dependent on an internal clock marking real time, that same musician should be able to take over when the power goes off at the Naval Observatory—in a laboratory he should be able to listen to precisely timed intervals and tell us their duration, or produce a sound of specified duration when we ask him to. Alas, he does not. Even when asked to perform this task using test durations commonly played in music, his performance is neither better nor worse than that of Uncle Irving.[1]

Conceivably, the musician's special rhythmic skills might derive from an internal clock that operates outside conscious awareness. We might flush out this silent clock by demonstrating some sort of intrinsic rhythmic activity in the brain itself, then establish a linkage between that activity and the temporal aspects of some sort of motor behavior. This theory would predict that musicians will be found to have electrical rhythms, or rhythmic precision, in their brains lacking or diminished in others.

As it happens, there are indeed a variety of rhythmic electrical events in the brain, above and beyond the alpha waves mentioned earlier. We shall look at them, and their relations to muscular activity, but be prepared for a mild shock.

Neurophysiologists, psychologists, and neurologists encounter evidence of timed biologic events routinely in their work. In medical practice one sees people with involuntary shaking of head, arms, hands, or even tongue and soft palate. Electrical recordings of the muscles producing these rhythmic movements (tremors) show them to be driven by commands coming from the central nervous system. They are often clocklike in their regularity, and can persist at a stable frequency for years without interruption (except in sleep). Such abnormal movements might seem to unmask (if not precisely locate) an internal clock, because they proceed at a regular pace, unaffected by any identifiable timed events taking place outside the body. The ultimate source of these control signals, however, never appears to be in a single structure in the brain sending out time signals after the fashion of the phone company or the Naval Observatory. Instead, the situation seems to reflect an upset in the relationship between two or more regions in the brain which usually work in harmony to guide voluntary movement. In other words, the rhythmicity observed in these movements is just a physiologic (and usually disturbing) accident.

All we can safely say here is that there are normal physiologic mechanisms which proceed in a predetermined sequence, with at least some component steps requiring a specific time to complete. If such a sequence were interrupted during one of its timed steps, the cycle might be thrown back to a point preceding the break, to try again to run its full course. If the interruption amounted to a functional roadblock, the same thing would occur repeatedly, producing a new and functionally abnormal cycle.*

Sometimes we see another rhythmic form of brain activity controlling bodily movement—I am referring to the condition known as epilepsy.

We noted earlier that the brain normally produces some rhythmic electrical patterns, like the alpha waves. But these are not produced by any command signals known to drive the body's muscular system. In epilepsy the rhythmic waves are *abnormal,* and the body responds to them in a variety of ways. For a period of time that is usually very brief (seconds to minutes), all movement may cease; twitching or jerking movements of some part of the body (or the entire body) may occur; attention may be impaired, or consciousness may be lost.

One of the most interesting of the many forms of this disorder is called petit mal epilepsy. This is a condition that affects many young people, and is characterized by brief periods during which awareness of the surroundings ceases; during this time all meaningful activity is also interrupted. To an observer, the person having such a spell appears to be in trance.

Petit mal is not a disease; rather, it appears to be an occasional disturbance in normal brain function due to a delay in maturation of part of the brain (the disorder normally corrects itself spontaneously during adolescence). During an attack, the electroencephalographic tracing shows normal brain electrical activity to have been usurped by machinelike three-per-second waves, which are recorded over its entire surface. When the abnormal brain

*This is one of the problems you can have with phonograph records: The needle can't get past a pothole in the groove, loses a lap, and tries again, and again, and again. The rhythm you then hear is not that of the song you're listening to but that of the record player counting out the time of the single revolution where it is trapped. Any rhythmic tremor in the body could easily be produced in this way.

waves disappear, normal consciousness and activity instantly resume. Not only is it unclear why the abnormal activity begins—it is not known why it stops.

There is a disquieting trend shaping up here, well worth pondering. Evidence points to an inference that the brain is certainly capable of running the body's voluntary muscles in a highly rhythmic pattern, but only does so when something has gone awry. That *is* odd—is musical skill a disease?

Do not despair; the biologists may be at a loss for the moment, but unexpected twists are the ultimate delight of the true scientist. Moreover, the paradox begs for exploration by the joint efforts of biologists and musicians. What could be more enticing than a research project using music to study some of the knottier issues of human behavior? In particular, it would seem that a closer look at the timing of musical events could give us a novel slant on the physiology of timing in the body.

You will recall that it has been found that musicians are no better than anyone else at guessing the duration of a brief sound, even when it lasts about as long as a common musical note. On the other hand, they are remarkably good (better than nonmusicians) at reproducing rhythmic sequences that they hear. What does this set of findings imply?

The musician's undistinguished sense of *absolute* time compared with a heightened sense of *relative* time suggests that our thinking may have been swayed by examples of real clocks running machines. Is it possible that biologic clocks can control timing without a centrally generated reference signal? What would that mean for musicians, basketball players, or high hurdlers?

If rhythmic accuracy is not dependent on an inner pulse, or clock, there is only one other way to explain it. It must have something to do with the way the command system running our movements parcels out relative durations of moves in a sequence at the time they are learned. This may sound obscure, but it really isn't. All it requires for illustration (and clarification) is the example of highly skilled movements seen outside a purely musical context. We need to find a pianist who is playing something that isn't music; are there any secretaries who would care to step forward? Please bring your typewriter.

Psychologists have been interested in typists for a long time, for a number of reasons. For example, they are able to produce written text at a faster rate than can be accounted for on the basis of their ability to react to letters of the alphabet seen one at a time.* Moreover, the speed any typist attains can be severely impeded by limiting the amount of text that can be seen in advance of the letters and words being typed. You can also slow down production by presenting nonsense words to type, or words with the letters in reverse order.

The conclusion most people reach when looking at these data is that typists gain speed by building up strings of letters which have meaning and can be treated in their grouped form as though they were a unit. This transformation of individual letters into larger cognitive units is called "chunking." The larger units can be words, phrases, or even sentences that are familiar. Not everyone agrees that efficiency develops by this mechanism; if you're interested in exploring this topic there is a concise review in a recent *Scientific American.*[2]

When you look closely at the *output* side of chunking among typists (that is, at the way they actually perform familiar sequences with their machines), you see a few startling details, some of which are of great interest with respect to questions on rhythmicity, timing, and elusive biologic clocks.[3]

One such study of typists found that common words are typed as though made up of notes to be played in a strict rhythmic

*There is an important practical lesson for musicians in this, which is reviewed in the chapter on sight reading.

pattern. Were we to gather fifteen examples of the word *florist* or *government* typed by one individual, and record the time to type it on each occasion, we could express the length of time elapsed between each component letter (*f* to *l*, *l* to *o*, *o* to *r*, and so forth) as a percentage of the total time required to type the entire word. On a slow day, a typist might take 1.5 seconds for *florist* and 2.5 seconds for *government*, and on a fast day type both in half this time. Time required for the remaining thirteen productions would fall between the slowest and fastest values for each word.

Next, we could convert the letter-to-letter elapsed time to a percentage of the time required to type the whole word, and see what proportion of the total is taken by each interval in the word on each of the fifteen trials.

Doing this, one finds that experienced typists are highly consistent in the time ratios each interval consumes regardless of their overall speed. Which is what I said before: They "play" the letters as though they were rhythmically scored.

Apparently this patterning is so stable that it is almost possible to identify individual typists by looking at the rhythmic patterns that occur when they type any given word. The significance of this quirk of typists looms large when we look at another timing study of performance, in this case of pianists.

Using special equipment to record the time of hammer movement, scientists can now obtain and analyze the timing of pianists with great precision. This has been done with individual performances and with duets. One such study included the analysis of pieces from the classical literature played on two occasions, a full year apart. The findings were astonishing to the investigators:

> The analysis of piano playing made in our laboratory included a performance of a Chopin study. This study is an exercise in playing a polyrhythm in which the right hand plays three notes

> of equal duration in each beat interval while the left hand plays four. Thus the motor system has to compute different subdivisions of a beat interval for each hand. In the performance the division of beat interval was modulated by two kinds of expressive variation of timing, one affecting tempo and the other the synchrony between the hands. . . . The pianist returned a year later and gave two more performances of the same piece. The performance was analyzed to see whether there was a clock controlling the timing. The odds were felt strongly against this result because the large amount of rubato (intended change in tempo) suggested spontaneous expression of feeling rather than concern with musical architecture. It seemed unlikely that the same pattern of expression would be generated on occasions so far apart in time. . . . In fact the graphs showed a high degree of consistency between all three performances. Thus, contrary to immediate impression, these were highly crafted performances based upon the architecture of the music.[4]

In other words, the piece was played by the pianist the way typists type: with a degree of rhythmic consistency so precise as to constitute a personal signature. What does this tell us about rhythm and the clock?

It tells us that when we learn a sequence of moves which we execute as a unit, musical or otherwise, we specify not only the sequence but the timing of the component moves. The clock here is not a duration computer but a *proportion* computer. It operates in a complementary fashion with the other clock, which measures the beat, and it parcels out the events between beats in a manner that satisfies the composer's rhythmic intent, no matter how slow or fast the piece is being played. The rhythm, in other words, is specified in the motor program which guides the sequence of moves, and will be just as stable as the moves themselves are.

Even though this representation of the physiology of musical clocks is only an educated guess, it seems to me to explain two common experiences of musicians and does so in what scientists refer to as a parsimonious way—it makes sense and isn't too far-fetched.

The first experience has to do with the discovery of musicians that they are sometimes able to play a piece of music virtually error-free after (in some cases) not having seen, heard, or played it for a period that could be as long as years in duration. It is inconceivable that one could resurrect and reproduce a rhythmically correct version unless the instructions for rhythm were imbedded in the instructions for sequence. If the musician rehearsed the piece often enough to be able to play it after an interval of years, he also rehearsed the nuances of expression and learned those as well as the notes themselves.

The second experience has to do with the dissociation between tempo and rhythm frequently experienced by performers playing in a state of excitement. Any musician who has publicly performed music with technically difficult fast passages will report occasional astonishment on hearing recordings of these performances, revealing a tempo "much faster than I can play it." The ability to perform accurately at speeds never rehearsed has one extremely important implication, and supports the notion that rhythmic execution is not controlled by a clock measuring real time. If the command signals from the brain permit rhythm to be controlled independent of tempo, these two "unified elements" of music must be regulated independently. As a result, if the notes are secure, the execution can be as fast as is consistent with the mechanics of the instrument and the hand (or lip/tongue/vocal cords/diaphragm).

It is a good thing for us that our physiology is arranged this way, because musical effect is critically dependent on rhythm just as much as it is on tempo or melody. In fact, in any situation in which tones are being blended, the perception of melody may be critically dependent on rhythm. Douglas Hofstadter, who wrote *Goedel, Escher, Bach,* describes his experience learning the Chopin Etude in F Minor:

> After a couple of months of practice my fingers had built up enough stamina to play the piece evenly and softly. This was very satisfying until one day an acquaintance for whom I was playing it commented, "But you're playing it in twos—it's supposed to be in threes." I looked at the score and, as she had pointed out, the melody was written in triplets. But surely Chopin had not meant it to be played in threes. After all, I knew the melody perfectly. Or did I? I tried playing it in threes. It sounded strange and unfamiliar, a perceptual distortion the like of which I had never experienced. [I then listened to a recording by the pianist Alexander Jenner, who played it so smoothly and so free of accent I found I could hear it either way.] All of a sudden I saw I knew *two* melodies composed of the same sequence of notes. It was like falling in love with the same person twice.[5]

Hofstadter, happily, saves us from the dry and mistaken conclusion that rhythm is just fractions. He also brings us to the first of several points I feel must be made to bring all of this home, and to make it useful to you.

First, as already noted in the chapters on auditory perception (and recently emphasized by composers of electronic music), our perception of pitch has a great deal to do with the duration of the sounds we are exposed to. The more closely we look into our perception of music, the more closely entwined pitch and rhythm become.

Second, we have long taken for granted that music's force resides as much in its tempo—its overt breathing and pulsation—as in its melodic expression. But as we come to realize the degree to which melodic perception depends on rhythm, and at the same time to realize how much rhythm itself has to do with skilled movement, we are brought to the threshold of a more subtle (and, for me, more exquisite) theory. Perhaps the extraordinary evocative *range* of music stems from its ability to suggest earlier movement histories which hold meaning for us—that is, to revive the steps of what might be called a former dance. In any case, we must grant that we feel music through its remarkable effects on our movements as much as through its profound (and mostly unobservable) effects on our brains.

For me, as a neurologist, there seem to be no answers, just more questions. I will share two of them with you.

First, I wonder why it is, really, that we react so remarkably to musical pulse and rhythm. Does the musical beat synchronize itself with the cardiorespiratory system and thereby harmonize, as it were, with the brain? Or does it happen because the timing of events in the brain is overwhelmed by invading rhythms that have broken into the inner sanctum through the ears? Is the auditory system a sort of neurologic Achilles' heel?

Second, have we stumbled onto a new way of thinking about musical memory? Is it possible that it resides largely (or even exclusively) in the circuitry by which the brain represents and oversees directed movement? The same question can take the form of a conjecture that musicians will appreciate, namely that muscle memory *is* musical memory (even though it's mostly in the brain).

A few concluding remarks will perhaps counteract whatever tendency the foregoing may have had to leave you feeling slightly adrift. All we've really said is this:

1. No matter how incoordinate you may have felt in contests (real or imagined) with others at any time in your life, you could not recognize "Three Blind Mice" if you lacked the equipment to process sequential auditory information and to register accu-

rately the onset times and durations of its melodic constituents. In other words, you are no more time deaf than you are tone deaf.

2. The physiologic system at your disposal for reckoning time is highly sophisticated, and intimately connected with neurologic systems active in emotional experience and in the control of highly skilled movements. Whatever natural musicality we display is in large part due to these neurologic relationships.

3. As a practical consequence of the above, it must be a paramount principle of musical study that you incorporate rhythmic accuracy into the practice of any music you are attempting to learn to play skillfully. The rhythmic patterns you practice will be as deeply set in your memory as the melody, and extremely difficult to alter once in place. Inattention to rhythmic precision is as serious a mistake for musicians as it is for people who tap dance, play Ping-Pong, make pizza dough, or juggle chain saws.

In a deliberate lapse from my intention not to masquerade as a music teacher, I would like to stress what I see as the benefit of clapping or singing out rhythms in order to build a rhythmic library in your auditory memory. It seems simple-minded, but the practice is commonly recommended by teachers of beginning students because it works. Unless you do this, you will forever languish in fourth grade, tearing your hair over fractions. Fortunately there are any number of beginning music books that have these exercises in them. Go to your music store and look for something with puppies, chipmunks, or bunny rabbits on the cover![6] Tell the clerk it's for the little prodigy at home.

Notes

1. Saul Sternberg and Ronald Knoll, "Perception Production and Imitation of Time Ratios by Skilled Musicians," *Annals of the New York Academy of Sciences* (1984), 423:429–441.

2. Timothy Salthouse, "The Skill of Typing," *Scientific American,* February 1984, pp. 128–135.

3. C. Terzuolo and P. Viviani, "Determinants and Characteristics of Motor Patterns Used for Typing," *Neuroscience* (1980), 5:1085–1103.

4. Henry Shaffer, "Timing in Musical Performance," *Annals of the New York Academy of Sciences,* 423:420–428, 1984.

5. Douglas Hofstadter, "Metamagical Themas," *Scientific American,* April 1982, pp. 16–28. The sentence in brackets is a paraphrase of Hofstadter's original.

6. Frances Clark, Louise Goss, and David Kraehenbuel, *Time to Begin,* Summy-Birchard, 1960.

9

Those Dark Spots in Front of Your Eyes Are Notes

ON SIGHT READING AND OTHER WAYS TO HUMBLE YOURSELF

After four years of studying the piano I began to wonder why I was still such a lousy sight reader. I was able to play moderately difficult short pieces from memory, but could not read through the simplest music without feeling taxed to the limit. Just looking at the music gave me a headache and a sore neck. When I asked my teacher about this problem, she told me that it was more important to play well than to read well, and that I should stop worrying about it. She reassured me that this was a skill that would inevitably improve with time; if I wanted to work at it, her advice was that I find some simple pieces to play, go through them without stopping, and not try to correct mistakes.

Almost all teachers advise their students to improve their sight reading this way, apparently because the strategy works. Charles Cooke urged the adoption of this plan in his delightful book *Playing the Piano for Pleasure,*[1] and provided a host of practical suggestions which I feel sure apply equally to the study of music written for any instrument.

Regrettably, having heard this advice, I was swayed by the opinion that reading was not really all that important. I could follow the path of least resistance as well as anyone. It was not until about a year ago that I began to think about the matter again.

At that time I met Rita Fuszek, professor of music at California State University, Fullerton. A pianist and authority on piano literature,[2] Professor Fuszek is a lady who takes reading seriously. When I confessed to her that I *hated* to read and was uncontrollably jealous of musicians who did this with ease (my wife, daughter, and son, for example), she just laughed. "The truth is," she said, "that there are great numbers of pianists who have the same feelings, and whose sight reading and *sight playing* abilities have failed to keep pace with the rest of their skills. You're not alone."

She said it was important to distinguish between sight reading and sight playing, because they involved different skills. Sight reading is looking at a musical score and being able to tell what's on it. In order to do this, you have to understand musical notation (key signature, note values and positions on the staff, musical meter, and something about musical theory). This ability is developed most rapidly by writing music, and leads to a level of recognition in which the eye takes in groups of notes according to their musical relationships, rather than one at a time. Musical analysis becomes a guide to the act of seeing, and they proceed together. Eventually you look at the page and hear ("audiate") it in your head. Composers and conductors could not function without this ability.

Sight playing is a bit different. This has to do with the ability to execute what is on the page with whatever muscular responses are required to get sound out of one's instrument. When it is done well, it is smooth, accurate, and in tempo, at the time of the first encounter with the score. "Accompanists are always *very* good at this," she said. Obviously, sight playing is built on sight reading.

Her interest in reading skill comes from her love of the piano literature. There is an enormous amount of music in libraries, much of it unread and unplayed because people lack the necessary skills to explore it. It isn't so much that all this music deserves to be played. But musicians with an aversion to reading deny themselves access to whatever written music they would discover only by exploring the music library.

She described a test she and colleague Robert Unkefer had developed to measure competence in sight reading and sight playing. After testing several hundred pianists they had a remarkable set of findings. First, as mentioned earlier, a high level of playing skill did not guarantee proficiency at sight reading and sight playing. Second, proficiency in sight playing was always related to economy of eye movements. Good sight players keep their eyes on the music, and poor sight players are constantly shifting their gaze back and forth between the keyboard and the music. The implication couldn't be plainer: In order to play music at sight, the student must develop a way to keep track of fingers and music without having to *look* to find out what is going on. C. P. E. Bach, Rita told me, had come to the same conclusion in 1722. His advice then: If you want to improve your sight reading, practice in the dark!

She routinely advises students to follow Bach's advice, to which she adds her own: Play memorized pieces and practice scales and arpeggios with eyes closed. Do the scales and arpeggios in all keys this way. Copy a few uncomplicated pieces and try to hear the pitches as you write them down. Learn something about basic music theory. These and other thoughts on this subject have been published in a series of magazine articles which you might find of help.[3]

I took part of the test. She counted 261 needless gaze shifts in 26 measures ("You are using your eyes to replace your sense of touch"); out of 554 notes played, I made 53 errors, about evenly divided between left and right hands. On 90 occasions I took another stab at a note I had already played (this is called stuttering), even though the first note was incorrectly played only 13 of the 90 times. Finally, it took me just over 13 minutes to play through the test. ("This is slow, but it is the movement of the eye, back and forth from the page to the keyboard, that is slowing you down.") She cited another pianist she had tested, a graduate student in a music program with numerous concert performances to her credit, who had taken over 20 minutes to play through the test. Obviously, we were both candidates for an overhaul in the sight playing department.

The more I have thought about this reputedly commonplace problem, the more I have felt it worth exploring in this book. What is it about sight reading and sight playing that gives people fits? Why do some pianists get along just fine without having to *see* what their hands are doing? Could it possibly have something to do with the brain, and the way we see? It would seem that eye movements really must have some bearing on this issue.

In order to approach what is (you guessed it!) a large and fascinating question, we should be aware that the analysis naturally divides itself into three segments: First, how does the visual system extract information from the environment? Second, what is the character of information available in a musical score? Third, how can we, or *should* we, organize and monitor our execution of a musical score on first encounter?

Let's take a look at the visual system first, to get an idea of its basic operating characteristics. You must understand that human visual perception has long been and continues to be the subject of intense interest and research in physiology and psychology laboratories. As with auditory perception, there are more questions than answers, and absolutely no studies that record the exertions of brain cells in humans making their way through Bach fugues or "Three Blind Mice." What follows can therefore be neither comprehensive nor authoritative, but it might make you more attentive to your own vision, and perhaps more patient with yourself as you set eyes and brain to master music's secret visual code.

The eye is not unlike a camera. It is a dark chamber with a small opening in front, through which light enters. The opening is covered with a transparent window, the cornea, behind which is a flexible lens. Both of these structures alter the optical behavior of light passing through them, so that objects will be in focus no matter how close or far away they may be. This neat trick is made possible by a circular muscle around the edge of the lens, which can stretch it into a flatter shape and alter the distance at which it brings light from a point source back into focus.*

At the focal point, the light makes contact with a photosensitive surface. In a camera, the light falls on the film you have loaded, where it causes a reaction to take place in the chemicals on the film; in the eye, it falls on a special structure called the retina, where it causes a chemical reaction to take place in a complex organic molecule called rhodopsin. There are several different forms of rhodopsin, each most sensitive to a particular color (blue, green, or red), but light causes all of them to bleach, which starts the ball rolling in vision.

The retina, like the cochlea, is an energy transducer. The brain cannot respond to energy in the form of light, so the retina has to convert light energy to electrical impulses. Cells called rods and cones begin this process, when the pigment they contain undergoes its bleaching reaction. Other cells in the retina amplify the reaction, and notify the brain of the arrival of light by way of a large nerve called the optic nerve. The main receiving station for this information is in the back of the brain, called the occipital cortex.

Now that we know how light becomes energy that can be used

---

*Your friendly optometrist can explain to you why this stops happening after you hit forty, and can provide you with the help you need to be able to make out the notes (and the newspaper, and the phone book) once again.

as information by the brain, we must ask ourselves how it becomes *useful* information. Just as the brain must sort through the impulses generated by sound, it must have a way to classify and selectively use visual information.

This brings us to an important difference between energy in the visible and in the audible spectra. As we learned in the earlier chapters on hearing, sound waves are produced by the compression of air molecules; they are audible to most of us at frequencies between 15 and 20,000 cycles (or vibrations) per second. Light waves are *not* made of air molecules, but they still can be described in terms of wavelength and frequency. Light waves are visible to us when their wavelengths are between 385 and 760 nanometers (billionths of a meter).*

We should stop here for just a moment to clarify a point about numerical descriptions of things. Depending on the size of our measuring stick, we can attach a number of almost any size to anything we want to measure. You, for example, might be described as five feet tall, sixty inches tall, or .000947 miles tall. You are the same size in each of these examples, but by changing the unit of measure we can compare your size to that of something else of interest.

A curious thing seems to have happened with our conventions for measuring light and sound; in each case we have adopted a scale whose basic unit is virtually the same as the size of the smallest difference humans are able to detect. Most of us can hear (or can be trained to hear) differences in sound waves that

*We use the term *wave* to refer to a certain kind of repeated or periodic motion. We may be looking at a hair wave, an ocean wave, a sound wave, or a light wave. It really doesn't matter what it is or how fast it happens to be moving—when it moves in that familiar up and down or back and forth pattern we can measure the distance between successive peaks of the wave as well as the number of peaks that sail past us each second. These we call respectively the wavelength and the frequency of the wave.

are as small as one cycle per second, and can see differences in light waves that are as small as one nanometer.

Even without breaking your pencil over the details you can see that the number of individually perceptible sound frequencies is quite large (19,985) compared to the number of individually perceptible wavelengths of light (375). In other words, there is a huge difference in the capacities of sound and light to convey information by spectral position alone.

This disadvantage for light as an information-carrier is compensated by the difference in the speed with which light and sound waves move. For sound moving in air at sea level, that speed is a leisurely 0.2 of a mile (roughly a couple of blocks) per second. Light, by contrast, travels 186,000 miles (give or take a block) in the same period of time.

The reason for bringing this to your attention is to make it clearer than it might have been before just why eyes and ears are not built and do not operate in the same way. Thinking about the adaptation of anatomy and physiology to the idiosyncrasies of the physical world is not a bad way to get your psyche unstuck from the gravity of monthly car payments and other troubles. It might lead you even one step further, to appreciate the miraculous nature of perceptual equivalence. The brain hears a moo, or sees something brown with a particular color and shape, and gives you the same name: cow. This is no small trick.

Long before scientists began to trouble themselves with these weighty issues the Architect of our perceptual systems may have determined that frequency difference wouldn't be such a hot way to distinguish the light bouncing off trees from the same light bouncing off grizzly bears. But since these same light waves go so fast, and travel in a straight line, there would be another way to identify their source. This would require keeping track of where they land on the retina. In that way we would know at least where they came from relative to ourselves, and by analyzing the visual footprints we might be able to say *what* the source was. This last bit of detective work would require only the ability to measure very small distances on our receptor surface (the retina) accurately, a technique for gathering a few measurements very quickly, and a place to store and compare this information with similar kinds of visual information we had obtained about other things we had seen in the past. In effect, we might be able to construct a mental picture of objects giving off light within our field of vision, and see how closely it resembled the other pictures in the family album.

How might this actually work? Before we get to that question, we need to spend just a moment with the capacity of the system to alert us to possible danger, and to trigger protective reflexes even before we know what the danger is. The design of the retina itself provides a suggestive clue about the nature of the system we must employ.

The retina has two types of cells which contain photosensitive pigment. These are the rods and the cones, distinct in both their cellular physiology and their role in vision. The rods are maximally sensitive to green light, and the cones to blue, green, and red light. The cones are highly concentrated in a small region (only a fraction of a millimeter in diameter) directly opposite the pupil, called the fovea. In the center of the fovea no rods are found. The remainder of the retina has a mixture of rods and cones. Because of this arrangement, color discrimination is best for light falling on the fovea.

Resolution of small detail, or acuity, is also best at the fovea. This difference is thought to be explained by the connections of many rod cells to a single amplifier cell, in contrast to the isolated, single connections of cones to such cells.

The arrangement of rods constitutes the structure for an extremely effective visual warning system. Light falling anywhere on the retina, no matter how far out on the periphery, will activate the network of rods at that point on the retina and signal the presence of a target. The faster the object is moving, the more cells in this network will be activated. The result (thanks to a highly efficient system of reflexes involving the eye muscles, and the muscles of the head and neck and rest of the body) may be to cause you to turn head and eyes toward the target, blink, and perhaps duck, all at the same instant.

The peripheral system is designed not only to detect light but to tell us quickly where it is coming from and (crudely) where it is going. Because of the geometry of the retina, and the optical behavior of light, the image of an object above you will fall on one part of the retina, while the image of objects below, or to the left or right, will fall respectively on other localized regions of the retina. In other words, *location* of peripheral retinal activity is a code for locating any target in space, relative to your body. Simple, but fast and reliable; it's just what you need if you live next to a golf course.

For this to come to your aid when it would be healthy to duck, the brain must have a system with some of the same capabilities of radar navigation systems. It must be able to locate objects and guess their course and speed in order to predict whether you are on a collision course or not. Although there are any number of ways this could be accomplished, the system probably depends on special cells in the brain wired up to react only to visual stimuli moving in specific ways. They don't just react to light; they react to *oriented* light. The details of this linkage are stupefyingly complicated, so we will just express our wonder and gratitude, and move on.

At one time it was thought that the brain manages to identify a light source, after having located and tracked it, mainly by relying on the geometry of the retina. As with a camera, the light coming from the object you are looking at creates an image when it is focused on the retina. It has the same shape and the same detailed features, smaller but in correct proportion. If you are looking at your Uncle Irving, as you have many times in the past, you are able to compare the current image with the stored memory of earlier visual impressions. If the essential features match, you've got him pegged.

This is the Gestalt theory, first suggested as a general principle of perception by the German psychologist Charles von Ehrenfels in 1890, and applied specifically to vision by Koffka in 1935.[4]

In a nutshell, it was held that your Uncle Irving had certain intrinsic features, a certain "Irvingness" which you learned to recognize as a whole. A banana looks like a banana sideways and end on because of its intrinsic characteristics, and for the same reason your Uncle Irving looks like Uncle Irving even when he's standing on his head. The pattern of his image on your retina matches the set of pictures of him you carry around in your head or your wallet, and you know who he is when you see him.

As is, this would be a burdensome system. You would have to have a mighty fat wallet with lots of pictures of Irving, and plenty of time to sort through the collection, to be able to pick him out of a crowd every time, winter and summer.

An alternative or modified version, faster and much more flexible, would be necessary to be effective in a visual environment with any complexity. Moreover, the system would have to be one capable of alerting you quickly when survival depended on your ability to respond to a threat before you could be certain exactly what it was.

If we were using the entire retina like a camera to take pictures of the world, deciding who was out there on the basis of resemblance, we would be in a real pickle. Suppose the visual target were actually the family dog (or, in my case, the cat). What a waste of time to go through all those other pictures before deciding we didn't have a match for Irving. And where would we be at that point? Where would we start looking next?

Apparently we *don't* use the entire retina to do this, at least in the way proposed by the Gestalt psychologists. It is likely we lean very heavily on the fovea, the part of the retina which gives us color information and fine detail. How, you ask, could we possibly squeeze the image of Irving, or anything else, onto that tiny spot and check it against our mugs gallery unless he were standing a mile away? Good question. And it leads us to the most interesting part of this story—one that should make us dizzy with awe at the visual tools we have been provided, and more hopeful at our prospects for success in sight playing (if we would stick with it).

We actually have a whole family of integrated visual systems, tailored to our needs and compatible with the physics of light and optics. As a consequence of the physiology of the retina and the brain, we react instantaneously to changes in lighting conditions, regardless of the magnitude of those changes; we adapt to changes in the size and distance of potentially dangerous objects we are inspecting, or recognize our idols instantly whether we see them in person, on television, in movies, or in the newspapers, standing still or in motion. As a result of the efficient collaboration of these systems, most of us have binocular vision, see in color, and can read poetry and dodge spitwads simultaneously without thinking we're doing anything fancy.

Since our vision does work in a coordinated manner, splitting it into functional components is only a device for helping us to understand the complexity of its operations. One such division I would like to review with you—peripheral and central vision—is particularly useful for our purposes because it brings us to a consideration of the role of the apparatus whose job it is to point the eye toward its target. This is the system of muscles responsible for movement of each eye, and the key to our understanding of how Uncle Irving can be squeezed into the tiny space occupied by the fovea.

As you know, our ears and eyes are all mounted in the head, and their orientation toward a sound or light source can be changed by moving the head. We turn to hear sounds more clearly, or to try to tell where they come from, and the same maneuver is used in vision.

The eyes, however, have an additional mechanism for movement which the ears lack: Each eye sits inside a socket (the orbit) and can rotate inside the socket because of a group of muscles attached to it inside the orbit. There are six muscles assigned to each eye, and they work in close cooperation to move the eye quickly to bring the image of a visual target over the fovea. They cooperate not only with the other muscles of the same eye but with those of the companion eye. Efficient use of the eyes demands (as much as possible) that the two eyes move as a yoked pair.

It might be supposed that the eye muscles are simply a device to keep the eyes pointed in the same direction, to avoid double vision: The failure of these muscles to work together usually *does* produce that problem. However, there is more to it. The eye muscles, it is thought by some, have a great deal to do with how you keep Uncle Irving on file visually.

The first inkling that things might turn out this way came as the result of a medical curiosity reported about fifty years ago. Prior to the use of antibiotic eyedrops, a significant number of babies were born with a serious eye infection, as the result of which their corneas became scarred and they were left functionally blind. An operation was developed which permitted correction of the corneal problem, and a number of individuals of a variety of ages had their "vision" restored. That was what the operation was expected to accomplish. What was restored, however, was not vision: only the eyes.

The newly regained eyes didn't work. People reported a chaos of light and shadow, which was mostly irritating to them. A familiar object placed in their hand was recognized by touch immediately, but could not be identified visually. Color identification became possible, and extremely crude light contrasts could be recognized. But picking out shapes was hopeless at first.

The critical clue was that objects remained strange even after they had come into focus. A black square had no "gestalt"; it was just an amorphous shape with corners. Subjects would learn how to identify a square by counting the corners, one by one. "Four corners means a square; this has four corners, so it must be a square. Four corners means a square; this has *three* corners so it must *not* be a square." And so on. Slowly, *very* slowly, the process of building up a library of things viewed under the guidance of a *precisely regulated sequence of eye movements* began to develop. And at some stage the counting of corners was done so quickly that it was no longer noticed. The person just "saw" a square, or another object.

Not surprisingly, some of the people just put their dark glasses back on and decided to forget it—it was just too much work!

The author of this extraordinary report came to this conclusion about the study: "The perception of visual space is a temporal process, and this is not only at the patient's first attempts to see, but also later, when the visual apparatus has so far developed that its effectiveness is scarcely distinguishable from that of a normally sighted person. However brief and automatic it becomes, the act of perception remains essentially unaltered in its temporal structure. The patient does not take in everything at once (though everything is given to him at once), but notices the mutual relation and contiguity of the separate parts. He perceives a succession of views forming part of a whole that he himself is obliged to create by shifting his gaze; in so doing, however, he becomes aware of the conjunction of the parts of the whole."[5]

Not everyone has agreed with this conclusion. The work can

be neither duplicated nor refuted, because infants are now treated at birth to prevent the infection. A variety of experimental techniques have been employed in recent studies of visual perception. These have included computerized analysis of eye movements, the use of reversing prisms, or special contact lenses to counteract the effect of eye movements, and studies of perception of complex material presented in brief flashes. Such studies have confirmed that eye movements have an important role in visual perception, without providing an explanation of the way they cooperate with the rest of the visual system to influence perception. Physiologic studies of these muscles themselves reveal them to be under the control of an exquisitely sophisticated guidance system, and able to generate an unusually large repertoire of fast and precise movements of the eyes. Given the general tendency of physiologic systems to be models of engineering economy, it would seem that all this high performance capability would constitute genuine overkill if the eye muscles were needed only to prevent double vision.

No one has yet managed to wrest the big answers about visual perception from Mother Nature—physiologists, psychologists, ophthalmologists, neurologists, optometrists, and physicists all have labored long and hard to produce a comprehensive theory, but there's too much territory. The questions just keep happily multiplying like all those buckets and mops in Walt Disney's *Fantasia*.

Will we ever fully understand visual perception? The chances of this happening are about the same as our being handed a comprehensive theory of political science. The fact that the business will remain unfinished for the foreseeable future need not deter us from seeking a few clues about the nature of visual skills in sight reading and sight playing.

Visual identification probably occurs because of an extremely fast and probably preprogrammed sequence of eye movements which successively fixate on what are called discriminant features. The specific features we search for in any case will depend on our general knowledge of the shape and inner details of most things in that same class. The more we know about what we are looking for, the smarter we are at picking out features that define it, and the more we tend to limit our search to those features alone. In essence, visual experience—thoughtfully engaged in—gives us a bigger and bigger number of sparser and sparser maps. These maps consist not only of the visual features of what we see and what we are looking for but the instructions to the muscular system that controls our vision and determines the sequence and type of information we use to make visual identification. That's *my* theory, at any rate.

If this is so, our internalized photo of Irving (and everything else) would not be a likeness in the Gestalt sense, but a composite of highly distinctive features to be scanned in rapid succession. "Outer edge of eye to subject's pupil is 3/8 total width of eye: (iris is greenish-brown); then up 30° to dark spot (mole) = Aha! *Irving.*"*

There are two things you might ponder about this system, and this kind of library. First, it is an active, seeking system. You see Irving because you already know what he looks like, and you *are* looking for him. If he is meeting you at the airport, you will find him no matter how awful the crowds are. If you are *not* expecting to see him, you could well miss him three tables away in a small restaurant (an oversight for which he might occasionally be grateful). Second, your immediate visual sense of Irving,

*In that connection, it is exciting to note that the part of the brain whose participation seems essential in the analysis and storage of spatial information (the parietal cortex) has recently been found to be extremely active in the control of eye movements during active search.[6] And then there is the matter of our dreams, which seem to occur only when the eyes are in motion (during so-called REM, Rapid Eye Movement, sleep).

full of rich detail, and seeming absolutely complete, is mostly memory. If he looks a little different to you, you take a closer look and inspect the whole face, checking details against the library. "Uncle Irv, you could use a couple of weeks in Florida, y'know."

Both the memory-driven and economy-of-search features of visual perception have been shown to have considerable bearing on music reading, the special nature of which we shall now consider.

Let's think now about written music, the notational system used to represent musical events on paper. You might want to have some music close by as we go through this, in case you are puzzled by anything I'm trying to describe.

In its most fundamental sense, music is written down to show you how to reproduce a pattern of musical sounds. Written music is merely a display of sound-symbols, whose final meaning becomes clear when you have done whatever is necessary to realize the sounds represented by the symbols. The process of realization requires a number of steps, the first being to turn those symbols into a plan for manipulating whatever instrument you use so that you and the instrument jointly will make the sounds that have been called for. The process of realization is not unlike that involved in using a typewriter to transcribe a written text, though in the case of typing it's not sound, but more text, that is being produced.

To do this, you must be familiar with the rules that govern the construction of two-dimensional maps of musical sounds. There are many such rules, and we will consider just a few.

At the simplest level, the reader discovers that the pitch of any note on the page is related to its vertical position on the staff. A gift from compositional tradition that makes this an easy rule to grasp is the placement of low notes low and high notes high on the staff. Pitch and eye ascend and descend together.

If you happen to be studying a keyboard instrument, you may also enjoy another apparent coincidence (or analogy), namely that the notes on the staff look like position markers for your fingers on the keys. Just looking at the music shows you where your fingers go.

Unless you are entirely new to all this, you realize that neither of these analogies is air-tight—once graduated from the wholesome simplicity of the key of C major, where most simple things are played on the white keys only, you find out how things *really* work. But there is no doubt whatever that these auditory and muscular analogues of what is seen on the page have a powerful influence on our responses to the notes on the page.*

Music can start with any pitch that can be played and heard. Since the pitch intervals between adjacent notes on the keyboard vary, the pianist, for example, is obliged to learn the rules for using black keys along with white keys when starting and finishing a piece on some note other than C. Doing this requires learning a separate notational system—sharps and flats.

Without going into details which are the subject of countless

---

*The seductiveness of this mode of assimilation was recently impressed on me by Eloise Ristad, a teacher who for some years had been puzzled by the occasional piano student who seemed unable to get the idea of notes as position markers. One day, acting on a combination of whim and hunch, she turned the music book 90° to the right for a student, so that the staff was now vertical. Now the low notes were to the left and high notes to the right, just as they are on the keyboard. The student reacted to this change the way some people react to their first roller coaster ride—she was all gasps and giggles over a new and thrilling sensation. Since Eloise thought others might be interested in this view of early music reading, she included a description in one of her books.[7] She found that after a few weeks (occasionally longer) of reading music sideways, the students who latched on to this gimmick made a rapid transition to the traditional orientation. One can't help wondering about dyslexia in the background of some of these students. Here, the process of reading is confounded by the apparent visual equivalence of letter shapes that become one another when rotated (e.g., b, d, p, and q).

musical texts, it will suffice here to point out only that this is a system of formulas for *ignoring* what the notes seem to be saying, and making substitutions here and there on the page. The beginning student tends to feel himself walking a minefield when first confronted with pieces in keys other than C major, and probably here first begins the bad habit of shifting the gaze away from the musical line to another place which tells how to avoid being blown up. Here he is not unlike Dr. von Senden's patients who laboriously felt their way along with the eyes in order to make any sense of the chaos in front of them. Eventually, with practice and more practice, it is no longer necessary to hesitate before playing each note to be sure it isn't one of the dangerous ones.

It is amazing what happens once this system is integrated into the perceptual process. Psychologists who have made a study of the reading skills of advanced musicians tell us, as did Professor Fuszek, that notes become grouped into clusters that are taken in all at once, and treated as a unit. Although the entire process remains a mystery, it looks very much as though musicians come to the point where they see a musical line as though it were a silhouette, and what is executed is the plan for translating its spatial contour into a musical one.

The most informative studies of this kind, I believe, are those done by John Sloboda. He presented accomplished musicians with the scores of uncommonly played classical pieces, which had been randomly sprinkled with notes which were in conflict with the musical structure of the work. Pianists who played this music not only failed to see the errors but tended to *correct* them as they played. Although these results might seem to suggest the musicians to have supernatural abilities, there is a simple explanation. They were so familiar with the rules of compositon and execution that they tended to line up notes mentally in advance based on what they knew *should* be there. As Dr. Sloboda points out, this process of unconscious substitution and correction is something we all do regularly. It explains the difficulties writers face trying to proofread their own manuscripts; because they are so familiar with the text, and so sure what ought to come next, they tend to overlook the actual errors.[8]

I wish I could say this was the biggest hurdle faced by the the hopeful sight reader. In my opinion, perceptually at least, it is not. Visually more simple than the tortuous and scattered signs for reading pitch, but far more treacherous in its inner workings, is the system for keeping track of time.*

I am indebted to Professor Jeanne Bamberger at the Massachusetts Institute of Technology for her illuminating illustration and discussion of the problem facing a novice who must learn to cope with music's formal way of representing rhythmic concepts. Any teacher who has forgotten what it is like to learn this game should read the paper from which the illustration is drawn.[9]

Bamberger collected a group of schoolchildren in a class and gave them this problem: She clapped a simple rhythmic pattern for them and asked them to imitate her. They had no difficulty with this purely auditory-motor learning. They were able to clap the same pattern back consistently, so that there was no doubt they "knew" what the rhythm was. She then asked them to write down any way they wished the pattern they had learned, so that they would be able to look at it after a long interval and be able to clap the pattern again.

The pattern *sounded* something like this:

1   1   111   1   111

---

*Did you catch the proofreader's error in the first sentence of this paragraph—"the the hopeful . . ."? If you *didn't*, it means you unconsciously fixed an error in the visual code you were processing. Nice going.

Or, if this seems unclear to you, I've made up a little jingle which suggests the rhythm:

I like franks and beans,
Oh, how I do!

When you inspect my notational system, you gain the impression that there are two groups of three short notes and three separated longer notes. This becomes quite clear when you clap it out in a way that follows the accents of the jingle. You may not realize that you are reading the space between notes to be a code for time. The vertical lines fall on an imaginary measuring tape, moving beneath your eyes at a constant speed. When the mark crosses home base, you swing. Player pianos use exactly this system—holes punched in a paper that moves at constant speed—to drive the mechanism which controls the striking of hammers against strings.

All this is entirely logical, consistent, and highly effective. Unfortunately, life is not so simple.

As Professor Bamberger points out, the kids (based on both age and experience) tend to fall into distinct groups in the way they decide how to write instructions for their own later use. Of the many interesting features of this grouping, the most significant indicated that some children were using a formal strategy for rhythmic notation (not unlike that employed in standard written music), while others appeared to be improvising a written method for capturing what they had experienced in carrying out the clapping task. The principal difference had to do with the way the third note in the first cluster of three was represented.

The children without a formal strategy devised a code much like the one I wrote, emphasizing clusters of events whose timing is specified on a linear scale, and in which the third note of that cluster is *visually* identical to the two notes preceding it.

The children who tried to impose a formal set of rules to the solution of the writing task knew that the third note of that group could not be visually the same as the first two in the group, because the *interval* between it and the succeeding note is not the same. This is precisely what the established rules of musical writing prescribe: In this case you must show the *duration* of the third note as double that of its predecessors. This way the onset of the next note is postponed until you want it played.

In truth, and this is especially true in clapping, the rules of notation do not reflect acoustically what is happening, because the duration of sound of all the notes is virtually the same (if you ignore accents—that's another subject!). The children with training, however, have learned how to ignore this conflict and to write the notes in a way that satisfies the double-entry book-keeping system. They use a notation which specifies duration, as the one I've made up here does (m = 1 count long, or, if you like, a quarter note; n = ½ count long, or an eighth note):

m m n n m m n n m

A notational system of this kind suggests visually that you are presenting claps in clusters of *two.* It is a system in which distance is no longer a code for elapsed time, so auditory and visual consonance has been lost.

Why give up a system that is so easily grasped, and that provides such an intuitive correspondence between visual and auditory perception? Blame the composers. The onset and duration of notes establish a piece's rhythm, and composers have to represent these aspects of tonal events in a way that can be uniformly understood without demanding that distance equal time. The second of these conditions is a necessity for the simple reason that a composer is legally entitled to include as many notes in a single measure as he wishes to. If they are to be of uniform size in print, the only way to avoid turning them into sardines is to move the boundaries of the measure to accommodate the entire population. When you do this, distance cannot equal time, and you have to code duration some other way.

The rational way to code for duration is to hang that information onto the note. In my system, you have to read only when the note starts. In the fancy system, you have to read when it stops as well.

This gets us back to physiology, and it means that the person reading music must use a forward-looking computational system which decides physical onset time and duration based on the proportion each note bears to others in the same measure.

Somehow you must process the visual signals through a specialized circuit which can decode and rewrite them in a language that the auditory and motor systems understand. This is not unlike what happens around April 15th each year. You can't just pay your taxes the way you did last year; you have to wrestle with a bunch of forms and calculations, and maybe send the whole pack of stuff off to an accountant, who will then *tell* you the bad news. After all this has happened, you can begin to move your trembling hand across the face of the check.

No matter what the fine physiologic details may ultimately prove to be, playing written rhythm requires at least a two-stage system of computation and translation. This is a distinctly different (and far more complex) way of controlling movement than that of the backward-looking auditory memory system which reads an external clock and paces movements to fall in step with it.

The beginning student learns to read rhythmic notation by computing fractions, and then (if you like computer terminology) accessing his auditory timing system by clapping or saying the sounds in a rhythmic way. In so doing, he is learning to fantasize the auditory expression of the rhythm which he is reading. Eventually, with practice, the notational system becomes so familiar that it can trigger the appropriate timed sequences without the necessity of working out the pattern clap by clap. In this case the musician behaves as though he had heard the rhythmic sequence and is now imitating it. This is a phenomenon that seems analogous to the advance in facility with written language, when the words can be heard internally as soon as they are seen.

If you are skeptical about the possibility that this sort of thing really does happen—especially to anyone past the age of seven—I invite you to consider the report of the late educator John Holt, who described one of his experiences along these lines:

> For some weeks I had been slogging my way through the first movement of the Telemann suite, one note at a time. . . . I had no idea what the piece sounded like. I had never heard Bill play it, had never heard a record of it, had never tried to sing or whistle it for myself. It was just black notes on white paper. One weekend I went down to visit my parents in Rhode Island. I got on the bus [and I began to hear in my head] a tune that I couldn't place, couldn't even remember having heard before. . . . The tune played on, and after a while I decided to relax and enjoy it. I had stopped wondering what the tune was, was hardly paying any more attention to it, when suddenly a voice inside my head said, "Hey! It's the Telemann! It's that flute piece you're supposed to be playing." . . . Clearly the unconscious musician in me, a far better musician than the conscious, . . . had decided for itself how it *had* to sound.[10]*

Near the beginning of this chapter, I suggested that we should proceed in three stages: an examination of the visual system,

---

*Other aspects of this same issue are explored further in the chapter on timing. You may want to look into Michael Montgomery's fine book[11] as a way of getting started, or at the Keilmann workbook[12] if your instument is the piano.

then a look at the character of the information available in a musical score, and finally the formulation of a strategy for organizing and monitoring our execution of a musical score on the first encounter. We have arrived at the last of these three stages.

It seems to me that anyone ought to be able to learn to sight read and to sight play, and that it makes good sense to take the trouble to learn. The recent studies of sight playing by accomplished musicians suggest that the skill develops in almost exactly the same way that the skill of prose reading develops. It is a slow process, because most of the time is spent molding abstract musical principles into versatile, high-speed physiologic operations. The phenomenal complexity of the process is such that we do not yet understand the control of muscular movements which direct the eyes in their role as sense organs; we are as far or farther still from understanding how the visual information thus acquired guides the motor system controlling the limbs so that the music called for by the score can be played.

With respect to the basic skill of reading alone, there is the semblance of a small piece of solid ground to stand on: Literacy with respect to a musical score is based on a strategy for simplifying and organizing the material.* All the evidence suggests we do this with a physiologic mechanism for reading contours, guided by rules for breaking unfamiliar text into subunits whose contours match others stored in our library.

Studies of skilled typists make it clear that the eye must be ahead of the hand in order for execution to proceed smoothly. There is no getting around this: You must know what you are looking for and be able to recognize it with minimal searching. I don't know how you can do this without understanding something of music theory (i.e., the basic rules of composition). If

---

*For an enlightening demonstration of such a strategy, see the section on sight reading in Seymour Bernstein's splendid book, *With Your Own Two Hands.*[13]

the study of a set of abstract rules sounds burdensome, there is another strategy which might be more appealing. Nowhere is it written that you can't get a basic text in composition and try your hand at it.

The fact that experienced pianists make proofreading errors when sight playing simply shows the degree to which notes are chosen by composers because the rules leave no choice. The experienced reader, and the experienced musician, learn to ignore redundant detail.

The extreme penalty paid for gaze shifts in sight playing seems to me to deserve special attention. I suspect that the delay caused by gaze shifting occupies a far longer time than is required simply to look down at the hands and then back up at the page. It seems very likely that that act interrupts a controlled sequence of eye movements needed to identify the contour being examined. The gaze shift hurts because it breaks up more than information flow: It breaks up information *content* as well.

The studies have not been done, but I'd wager that careful analysis of eye movements of pianists doing what I did on the Fuszek-Unkefer test would show that the eye returning to the page loses ground as well as time. In order to restart the analytic process, it is probably helpful to synchronize the whole system (visual and motor) by running briefly through a sequence that has already been successfully executed. I wouldn't be surprised if that turned out to be the reason for stuttering (at the piano).

It seems to me that there need not be an absolute rule against looking at the hands. Cooke, incidentally, maintains this in his chapter on sight reading. If such movements were coordinated with the music itself (just as singers do with their breathing), and planned to take place when phrasing permitted, they should not interfere with information flow or content, or the smoothness of playing.

The liberation of the eye from its job as a monitor of the hand should require little more than the simple steps recommended by those who have thought seriously about sight reading. Undertaking this task (which will require time and patience) should have a double benefit. It will develop visual memory and analysis; more than that, it cannot fail to encourage the auditory system in its role as an active and guiding listener.

I will remind you here (as do Charles Cooke, Professor Fuszek, and others) that you must not make the mistake of practicing the skill of sight playing on the music you wish to learn or to perform. As mentioned in the earlier chapters on the motor system, and reiterated in the final chapter of the book, the most efficient strategy for memorizing a piece seems to be one which proceeds in an error-free manner. When you are learning to sight play, the idea is to press on, never looking back at the awful mess you've made.

If you have the good sense to read Charles Cooke's book, you will understand my resolution to go out and rake some leaves! When that's done, I plan to apply for a research grant to study eye movements, and volunteer to be a subject. Anything for science!

Notes

1. Charles Cooke, *Playing the Piano for Pleasure,* Part Two, Chapter 5 (Sight Reading), Simon and Schuster (Fireside Book), 1960.

2. Rita Fuszek, *Piano Music in Collections: An Index,* Information Coordinators, Inc., 1982.

3. Rita Fuszek, Guest Essay Series on Sight Reading, *Keyboard Arts Magazine,* Winter, Spring, Autumn, 1977; Autumn 1983, Winter, 1984.

4. K. Koffka, *Principles of Gestalt Psychology,* Routledge and Kegan, 1935.

5. M. von Senden, *Space and Sight* (1932), transl. by P. Heath, Methuen, 1960.

6. R. Wurtz, M. Goldberg, D. Robinson, "Brain Mechanisms in Visual Attention," *Scientific American*, June 1982, pp. 124–135.

7. Eloise Ristad, *Bold Beginnings: Keyboard Discovery, Book One, Section Three* (Movement from Line to Space Notes), Dorian Press, 1975.

8. John Sloboda, "Music Performance," in *The Psychology of Music*, ed. Diana Deutsch, Academic Press, 1982, pp. 486–487.

9. Jeanne Bamberger, "Intuitive and Formal Musical Knowing: Parables of Cognitive Dissonance," in *The Arts, Cognition and Basic Skills*, ed. Stanley Madeja, CEMREL. 1977, pp. 173–209.

10. John Holt, *Never Too Late*, Dell (Merloyd Lawrence), 1978, pp. 125–126.

11. Michael Montgomery, *Music: A Step by Step Guide to the Foundations of Musicianship*, Chapter 4 (Music and Time), Spectrum, 1981.

12. Wilhelm Keilmann, *Introduction to Sight Reading*, transl. by Kurt Michaelis, Henry Lilolff's Verlag/C. F. Peters (English), 1972.

13. Seymour Bernstein, *With Your Own Two Hands: Self-Discovery Through Music*, Schirmer Books, 1981, pp. 40–45.

10

Show Time!

STAGE FRIGHT REVISITED

Implicit in the act of making music is the idea, or the possibility, of performing for an audience. Depending on our nonmusical experiences with life's endless opportunities for performances of one kind or another, our feelings about music-making in the spotlight might range from nonchalance to abject terror. Most of us who start music as adults see ourselves as performing occasionally for a few friends, or not at all. We have attended enough concerts in our lives to know we're not going to make it to Carnegie Hall or any other place where you pay good money to hear good music. The demands of a performance career are so obvious and so extreme that we are content to imagine what it might be like were we to venture into the realm of *real* musicians. Who would want to hear our stuff anyway?

Think back for a moment about the last time you had to face an audience; it may have been nothing more than offering a toast at a retirement party, or accepting an award at a club meeting. Maybe you got up in front of the school board and made a plea for a bigger budget for the arts programs in the school (good for you!); maybe you tap danced at an office party.

Unless we are in a job or profession that routinely demands appearances or presentations in front of an audience, we tend to forget that the fastest way to find out how securely we have anything in our grasp is to hold it up in front of an audience. Since most of us don't do this sort of thing regularly, the chances are good that we are more than a little shy about public exposure;

if we have learned any new skill, or are in a new job and feel shaky about it, we are not about to publicize our inexperience.

Despite the apparent hazards, though, it is a great mistake to refuse outright any sampling of this part of the musical experience. Most good teachers plan recitals for their students, regardless of age or state of advancement, and I don't think they do this because it is fun for them. On the contrary, the student recital is without doubt the most traumatic recurring event in a teacher's professional life. But it is done anyway. The reason, I believe, is that teachers know their students learn something preparing music for a recital or concert that they cannot learn any other way. The recital is a transparent threat (though a well-meaning and generally constructive one), which requires the student to make a real commitment. By a certain date, a particular piece of music must be in the best possible shape, because forty people (most of whom know you and can't believe you are really doing this) intend to come to hear you play it. The knowledge that this will happen creates a particular kind of excitement which, like pain, concentrates the mind wonderfully. It is a positive force for hard work and progress. It gets results; the strategy works in nonmusical situations, too.

The music student, regardless of ultimate goals, needs to be under the gun once in a while if there is to be much prospect for refinement of the music being studied, or of basic musical skills. A recital is usually preceded by the attempt to memorize the music, or some part of it. This effort almost always changes the way the music is seen, heard, understood, and played. Even if the music is not successfully memorized, making the attempt forces the student to pay attention to details that are easily overlooked when the intent is to play but not to learn it. When a piece *is* memorized, attention tends naturally to turn toward those details of interpretation that seem to be guided by the ear and sense of touch. The claim has been made, to put this in aphoristic form, that once you learn the notes you can begin to learn the music.

To assert the value of memorizing one's music, by the way, is not to gainsay the superb musicianship of the seasoned accompanist or studio or orchestra musician, whose attention is simultaneously riveted to the printed music and the behavior of a soloist, other musicians in the ensemble, or the conductor. Most of these musicians will themselves play from memory when they are the soloists.

So preparing for a recital is a tonic, or a spur of sorts, which ought to be part of the learning experience because it tends to bring the music along at a pace, and in certain artistic ways, which are of real value to the student. The pressure does it.

The problem, of course, is that students (and in fact all performers) experience this pressure in individual, sometimes unpredictable, and often overwhelmingly negative ways. Despite a teacher's calm assurances, feelings about the approach of the recital date can be marred by a growing sense of dread.

It may surprise you to hear that professional performers often feel the same way. So do tennis players, runners, and pole vaulters. Even after years of experience, a seasoned artist can feel the clouds begin to gather as soon as he thinks about stepping in front of a live audience. This prospect, as it looms larger, gives rise to a kind of dread that is very special to those who experience it. It is called stage fright, and it is rarely if ever eliminated by practicing longer or harder. Stage fright is a revolt of the entire body against a situation which resembles a trip to the gallows. And, as in the case of genuine executions, there is little that rehearsing can do to make one eager to appear as the main attraction.

Stage fright is not a form of rational anxiety, such as might occur when someone decides he has overlooked precautions he ought to have taken to avoid grief. Rational anxiety is a sort of sixth sense, and a useful tool for the wary. Stage fright, or performance anxiety, is not a tool but a state of general alarm, a loud and insistent warning to leave the country. And no matter how diligently the musician (student or professional) prepares for performance, it will tend to recur until something is done about it.

Physiologists have known for some time that we have a biochemical mechanism built into our body's endocrine system which mobilizes us physically when we need to protect ourselves, or flee, in order to avoid serious bodily harm or death. The discovery of such a threat (unexpected and imminent) sets off a complicated reaction over which we have very little conscious control; this reaction includes an increase in heart rate, breathing, and blood pressure, release of energy stores into the bloodstream, and diversion of blood supply to the heart, brain, and muscles. Clearly, all of these changes in body metabolism are beneficial in the face of mortal threat, since they bring us quickly to an optimal state of alertness, strength, speed, and metabolic efficiency. Thus aroused and primed, we were doubtless at one time well able to cope with the unexpected company of the saber-toothed tiger.

It appears that stage fright, physiologically, involves much the same process of metabolic activation as we employ for survival in any life-threatening situation. In marked contrast to the so-called "fight or flight" reaction, however, stage fright is not an advantage to those who experience it. There are a number of reasons why this is so.

The single most prominent biochemical event in the body's alarm reaction is the release of adrenaline. This powerful compound enters the bloodstream and is distributed to the entire body within a few seconds. Its effect on the brain is to turn all the lights on, full power, all at once. The body's larger muscles are supercharged. All this is providential when the task is to wield an ax or a club, or to take refuge in the upper branches of the nearest tree.

Musical performance is quite a different matter, however. In the first place, the psychological state should be that of alertness with absolute composure, allowing not only heightened but *selective* sensitivity to everything in one's presence. It is critically important for the musician to be able to fix, or shift, the focus of his attention at will so that he can adjust his playing to suit the immediate circumstances. A brain full of adrenaline is certainly awake, but not in optimal condition for making subtle distinctions.

A second difficulty arises because musical performance generally demands exceptional smoothness and precision of the movements used to produce sound from an instrument or the vocal apparatus. As we considered in an earlier chapter, it falls to the smaller muscles of the body to do most of this work. Flooding these muscles with adrenaline is like urging a mouse along with a cattle prod: The result is spasm and collapse. In short, the biochemical changes which are the hallmark of stage fright constitute involuntary self-poisoning by the musician.

Since stage fright represents a gross overestimate of performance as a threat, we need to consider how this mistake is made. If we could discover how to alter the performer's misconceptions about being on the stage, it should be possible to counteract the associated nervous response, which can be completely disabling. There is no simple answer, but there are undoubtedly some general principles that apply to most instances of stage fright.

The celebrated American composer Virgil Thompson wrote once that the idea of performance is actually a relatively new one in music, certainly less than four hundred years old. Music was not performed for public gatherings prior to that time; instead, it was either a mode of personal and private recreation, an intimate group activity, part of a ritual, or an accompaniment to dance.[1]

When Franz Liszt embarked on the world's first series of solo piano recitals, it was his intent to astonish audiences. No one prior to that time had ever had the temerity to suppose that an audience would sit still for a program limited to piano works performed by a single artist. This radical departure from tradition not only dramatized the independent stature of the piano literature but drew the undivided attention of the audience to the skill, or virtuosity, of the pianist. As he modestly put it, "*Le concert, c'est moi!*"[2] He changed the character of musical careers from that time forward. No longer was music just either a private recreation or a prized public companion to other activities; it had become also a vehicle for displaying the talents of the musician.

I think this is the crux of the problem with respect to stage fright. The possibility of failure can inspire real terror because musical performance, no matter how informal, has become an exhibition of musical skill rather than the event through which music is conveyed to or shared with an audience. Musicians have always been pleased when they play well, and grateful for the applause of an audience. But performers seem to work under a nearly obsessive preoccupation with the manner of execution of the music, as a result of which they are extremely vulnerable to worries about mistakes or failure.

Although the usual ingredients of the stage fright reaction are reasonably well known (the terror-prone individual, primed to react in a "dangerous" situation), it is not always easy to predict who will experience this problem, or in what circumstances. The most innocent-appearing situation can suddenly become menacing; a performer, or student, with no previous difficulty can be caught unawares and chopped up in a violent physiologic reaction that seems to come out of nowhere. The risks of performing are not unlike those of small-boat sailing in New England.

Let me tell you about my first experience with stage fright. Since I have long enjoyed speaking to audiences, and loved being in plays in high school, it had never occurred to me that I might have this problem. After my first bout, which was a real shock, I began to think about it as only a victim would. It happened at my first student recital.

There were about twenty of us on the program. Most of the pianists were far more advanced than I. My teacher, Lillian Cox, did not have any other beginning students—she had rewarded me with three free lessons in return for a lecture on the brain to her students. When it became apparent that I was hooked on the idea of learning to play, I was inducted into the program as a full-fledged student. This meant that I, too, had to appear in the student recital, six months off at the time I took my first lesson.

The lessons always went well, and I reaped endless praise for my diligence and progress. I even relished the time I spent practicing. It was all going swimmingly.

Once a month, in an evening session, the students were invited to attend a master class. There were occasional lectures given at these programs (I had given one myself), but mostly they were intended to be opportunities for the students to play for each other. Lillian regarded these as extremely important exercises for her students, providing them not only the opportunity to discover what others were doing but a small-scale recital experience as well. It was her strongly held opinion that such playing opportunities were essential for musical growth.

It was at my first master class that I discovered my own sensitivity to the performance situation. The piece I was to play was not difficult, and I had memorized it several weeks before the class. I had it clearly in my mind when I went to the piano. I also had in my mind that virtually everyone in the room had heard my "learned" address on the brain, and evidently a few complimentary reports about my early progress had made their way through the grapevine. Heed this, dear readers: It's wonderfully flattering to hear you can walk on water, but a bad idea to trust the rumor beyond the safety of your own bathtub.

Considering my preoccupation with my knees, which shook uncontrollably from the moment the first note sounded, it wasn't a bad performance. I didn't take this too seriously, and laughed about it as I confessed to the other students how it felt to be in this situation for the first time. In retrospect, I should have known there was real trouble ahead.

On the day of the annual student recital we were supposed to appear at the theater early enough to walk through our entry and exit, and to play a few notes just to get the sound and feel of the piano. I was late for this warmup, so my first encounter with the piano was when it was my turn to play.

I walked onto a stage which was formally set and found myself illuminated by a spotlight. This arrangement had a startling impact on my feelings about the occasion, since it signaled the recital to be considerably more stately and important than I had imagined it would be. All the other students were playing at a more advanced level than I, and it seemed obvious to me that I didn't really belong out there in front of all those unseen people, who must be expecting to hear a real pianist. I was sure I would flop, or at least appear ridiculous. The psychological stage was thus set for a bad outcome before I even sat down at the piano.

When I did sit down at the piano, which was a nine foot grand (I had never sat at the keyboard of such an enormous instrument before), it seemed to me that I was at the controls of a locomotive, a machine completely beyond my comprehension and highly unlikely to submit to my directions. At that moment my mind went blank, and I have absolutely no recall of anything that happened from that moment on while I was onstage. At the postrecital reception I was too distracted to wonder about the veracity of the uniformly positive comments I heard. Later I learned that some of the more sophisticated listeners had recognized what I was supposed to play.

At the first lesson following the recital, Lillian and I discussed what had happened. She was honest, objective, and reassuring. She insisted that I had done quite well, considering the fact that this was my first time out. She was sure that I would have profited from the walk-through just before the performance, since I had been so intimidated by the stage and the piano itself. And she cheerfully reminded me that the only real way to avoid stage fright, with its memory slips and so forth, was to "practice, practice, practice." This, in the final analysis, was the only way to gain the confidence necessary to play well in front of an audience.

So I practiced, practiced, and practiced. By the time of my second annual student recital, I was ready. And exactly the same thing happened again, only it was worse because this time I *didn't* go blank: Denied the merciful shroud of unconsciousness, I was forced to savor every moment. It was just the way I remembered in those early childhood dreams with steamrollers.

I think I would have abandoned all hope at this point, were it not for a truly remarkable comment made to me by a good friend who had witnessed the debacle; so far as I know, he was the only regular at these massacres who always had fun. I had already been awarded the obligatory postrecital smiles and handshakes by a few people when Bill came up. He looked me straight in the eye and said: "Well, Frank, you butchered it, but you were great!" This simple, honest, amused, and sympathetic comment put things right instantly, since it acknowledged both the effort and the accomplishment without denying what had actually happened. I have considered this remark many times to have been something of a beacon for my thinking and feelings about stage fright, because it prepared me to look openly at a variety of novel approaches to the problem which later came to my attention.

Since I was not the only student who came away from the recital in distress, I began inquiring of the others in greater detail about their feelings. Almost all of the students were afflicted with some degree of stage fright, frustrated by their inability to overcome it, and inclined to question their own good sense at repeatedly subjecting themselves to the trauma of performance.

The more I heard about this problem, the more I came to suspect that it was simply a universal part of the performing experience. It was also beginning to appear that the underlying sense of failure, or fear of failure, was somehow linked to the image of the musician as an acrobat, with every performance being the occasion for some kind of comparison with other acrobats.

The universality of this problem was finally brought home to me in the form of a question asked by a friend who is a touring concert pianist. He wondered what I knew about a particular drug rapidly gaining favor among concert artists and symphony musicians as "the cure" for stage fright. According to him, the reports of a few musicians widely known for their phobic attitudes on performance were nearly ecstatic: Some called the drug a miracle, and claimed that for the first time in their careers they were able to face live audiences with absolute calm. As a consequence of these revelations, and apparently within a very short time after the first news began to circulate, the story was that "everybody's taking it."

Propranolol, the drug in question, is normally prescribed as a treatment for certain heart and thyroid problems, for prevention of migraine, and for control of a mild form of shaking. A quick search of the medical literature revealed scattered reports of its use to treat anxiety, with cautious but nonetheless positive conclusions about it. There was even a report of an attempt to treat the anxieties of inexperienced helicopter pilots with it.

What is most fascinating about the drug is that it works in the body by blocking part of the biochemical system that produces the "fight or flight" reaction. Its success with musicians, therefore, adds weight to the argument that stage fright belongs to that class of primitive defense reactions launched by the part of the psyche that wants you to be around to enjoy your breakfast tomorrow morning.

Another interesting facet of the propranolol story was the sociological one; namely, that its use apparently became common among professional musicians in record time, and without the slightest encouragement from its manufacturer or the federal agency responsible for certifying pharmaceutical products for use in specific diseases and conditions. In other words, doctors could legally prescribe it for high blood pressure, and several other medical conditions, but not for stage fright. Since its near overnight success occurred despite the somewhat illicit circumstances of its use, it may be that the average performance career is even more arduous than has been generally supposed.

If the drug became so popular in such a short time because of its reputed effectiveness in stage fright, one would have to suspect that a significant number of professional musicians labor terribly under the stress of performance. And if this is true, it would seem to signify that there is something fundamentally amiss in music as we teach, learn, perform, and use it. The problem cannot be that all these people are not practicing enough. The problem must be that they are practicing the wrong way, or playing for the wrong reasons. Even if the pill makes it possible for them to endure the pressures of performance, in the long run it is not likely to make careers more satisfying. Because, as Adelaide in *Guys and Dolls* observed about Vitamin A and Bromo Fiz taken for the runny nose brought on by heartbreak, "The medicine never gets anywhere near where the *trouble* is."

I would like to emphasize to "late bloomer and nonprodigy" readers that we duffers have one clear advantage over our more talented musical idols. Those who must make their living at music, especially if they must do so with the problem of stage fright, have a much more pressing problem than ours. The stakes for them are very high, and the elimination of obstacles to success in their careers is a paramount concern. The butterflies we contend with, however mammoth, are still just butterflies.

I would like to return to the remark of my friend Bill. It was significant not merely because he managed to convey his encouragement without sacrificing his candor. It was even more significant because it defined his role as an active participant in the program, as a member of the audience. He was not there to pass judgment, keep score, bestow or withhold his approval. He was there to join in whatever happened, and to contribute his own feelings to the proceedings. The rest of us, I am afraid, were stuck fast in a vain enterprise, propping up the illusion that we were involved in some kind of test and could be proud of ourselves for that reason. Did some of the strain show through our smiles? I suspect it did.

Let me now describe what I regard as the escape route out of this predicament. It is a time-honored precept that music requires a composer (who conceives the music), a performer (who brings it to life), and an audience. We have no trouble seeing the essential parts played by the composer and musician in this formula, but it may not occur to us that the audience becomes an active part of the equation only *after* it has paid for its tickets and filled the seats.

In order to see that the audience is not really there just to pay the bills, it would help to set aside the familiar and obvious example of a major symphony orchestra presenting something like Beethoven's Seventh Symphony, or an appearance by one of the jazz greats like Ellington. Instead, try to imagine a sort of generic primitive setting for our concert—an American Indian village or a small Polynesian island would be about right.

In the time before musical performance became a vehicle for the display of the powers of the performer, music was probably most often presented in simple surroundings, as a means of fostering the closeness of small gatherings of people who were engaged in an activity meant to be set apart from their normal routine. Depending on the purpose of the gathering and the needs of those attending, the musicians might function in anything from an ornamental to a central role. Because of music's unique and immediate tendency to influence people's feelings and responsiveness, the musicians could even lead the gathering into a sort of waking dream, or trance, from which they might emerge serene, excited, happy, or sad, but in any case moved both by the effect of the music on themselves, and by the awareness of its effect on those around them. The musicians' skills included the ability to sense the mood of the audience, their needs, and their reactions to the music, and they could use this skill to heighten the emotional impact of the occasion. It should be apparent that in such a setting the musician would tend to feel in intimate contact with those around him.

Contrast this setting with what I found when I walked onstage for my first experience at a student recital. The surroundings were formal, not intimate, and the ceremonial trappings were deliberately arranged to create a feeling of separation between the performer (me, in the spotlight) and the audience (somewhere out there in the dark, on the other side of the border). The single word that best describes the performer's natural feelings in such a context is "isolation."

The separation between performer and audience is not promoted merely by staging, however. At most concerts and recitals there is a rigid protocol which decrees that the audience is to remain motionless and silent until the performance is over, at which time there is to be applause for a few moments, no matter what. In other words, the performer is *not* supposed to interact with the audience at all during the performance, or to know their true feelings.

The acclaimed pianist Lorin Hollander asserts that anxious performers tend to interpret the slightest noise coming from the audience as a sign of disapproval (a critic jotting down notes, or a conservatory student following the piece with a score, recording the missed notes!). Is it really a surprise that this situation should give rise to a sort of primal terror over danger lurking in the dark, and that our brain should respond by ordering up a fast dose of adrenaline just before the house lights go down?

Until recently, I would have thought the above reflections suitable as the basis for a lively discussion about stage fright, and the tribulations of the performance career, but not to have much value in suggesting or supporting practical solutions. That was before I met Eloise Ristad.

Several years ago I had the good fortune to receive notice of a book with the unusual title *A Soprano on Her Head.*[3] Intrigued with the title, I bought the book; fascinated with the book, I called its author. A piano teacher, she had become convinced that too many musicians were missing all the fun, excitement, and blossoming one would normally expect to be the natural reward for people in "creative" careers. More than a few with this problem were sinking deeper and deeper into anxiety, self-doubt, and depression over the failure of their life's work to satisfy them in any real way. Worst of all, these musicians tended to be least happy when they were onstage. Eloise had decided to try to help.

She suggested that I try to attend one of her workshops to see how she worked with musicians. I was able to do this, and the experience was a revelation.

If this workshop had a single theme, it would be described by the word "icebreaking." From the moment people began walking through the door, they were given things to do together. Juggling seems to be a staple in the early morning activities; it's lively, it's loose, and when about fifteen people are tossing balls in a small space you tend to get acquainted and unstuffy in a real hurry. Next, we learned each other's names, and there was a game to make *that* easy. We all offered brief biographies of ourselves, and we were as varied in our backgrounds, education, personal lives, and careers as any small group could possibly be. We had in common a strong interest in music and a collection of sweaty-palm stories to tell about being onstage (as rank amateurs and as seasoned professional performers).

The format for the workshop requires that everyone perform for the others attending—no exceptions, no excuses. Pefor-mances are usually brief, and are followed by a free discussion between the performer and the audience. Depending on what is disclosed during this discussion, some variation on the performance is devised, and it is done again. Almost invariably the performer will say he or she feels tense and uncomfortable. Eloise will not accept this description, pointing out that people experience tension in individual ways, and therefore some specific description of a physical symptom must be provided. The person may describe a stomach ache, a runny nose, a desire to jump out the window, or perhaps a feeling of suffocating. Whatever that symptom may be, it provides the clue to a dramatization of the problem.

In our group, a singer presented an aria from an Italian opera, and explained afterward that he had felt that his chest was tight and that he couldn't expand it enough to get all the air he needed. Eloise decided to have the singer and the rest of us explore that sensation as a group, and instructed all of us to surround him, placing our hands on his chest. He was to start singing again, and we were to press against him hard enough that he really *would* have trouble expanding his chest. He sang again for us, as we gave him some chest pressure, and when it was over we all had something to talk about. For him, it seemed that the feeling of constriction wasn't so bad, after all. For most of us, who had never had this kind of tactile contact with a chest full of the resonances of Italian opera, the experience was absolutely electrifying.

As each of us talked about what it was like not only to hear but to feel this music, it dawned on me that a very special bond was being created between the performer and his audience—we had become partners in his performance. We all sat down and he sang again. The change in him (and in us, I think) was impressive. After finishing he said he now felt our presence not only as positive (a novel experience in itself) but as somehow essential to a new feeling he had about the singing of the aria. In other words, we were contributing in some important way to the realization of the music itself. It is important to emphasize that at least half the members of the workshop were professional musicians. They were possibly the most startled witnesses to the transformation that took place as performer and audience rediscovered one another over the ensuing days of the workshop.

This kind of rediscovery is one way a musician (professional or amateur) can cope with the disabling effects of stage fright. And there are others: A variety of musicians share the opinion that the professional musical career may need a psychological overhaul. Help is becoming available in the form of counseling, or even formal psychotherapy, hypnosis, biofeedback, meditation, and several formally organized approaches having the status of "schools" (Alexander Technique and Feldenkrais Therapy, for example).

Over the past few years I have spent many happy hours discussing this issue with my good friend Jack Meehan, whose job it is to teach brass playing to the young members of a drum and bugle corps. Jack asserts that the real problem may come from the idea that rehearsal and performance are somehow different.[4] If we could think of music as a vehicle for the attainment of an altered state of consciousness, as was the case in the informal ritual I described earlier, we might be able to leave behind the image of performance as acrobatics.

For practical purposes, this means that the musician should incorporate into his practicing a continued sensitivity to the effect of the music on his own concentration, and should strive to use the music to improve this special sense of inner focus. When the musician comes to understand that he is practicing *only* for this purpose, he will begin to enter an altered state as soon as he begins to play, because he has disciplined himself to do so. And this will automatically happen whether he is alone in a practice room or with 127 other kids in front of a crowd of 30,000 people. I was recently reminded by a musical scholar that in many societies music is *primarily* used for trance induction, so perhaps this idea is really quite close to an important truth we tend to overlook in our relentless search for better and better acrobats.

What, finally, does all this mean? First, I think we must accept that music can profoundly affect people's feelings and their attentional focus, whether they are performing or just listening to it. We cannot explain this phenomenon, but we cannot deny it, either. Historically, and based on our own experience, we know music provides a special set of conditions when people participate in it together. If it is presented in a setting which separates the performer from his or her audience, there are risks that much of its potential effect will be blunted. The performer who feels isolated may begin to feel terrified by audiences and will ultimately feel cheated by music. Audiences gathered simply to witness demonstrations of virtuosity may find themselves out in the cold.

Music *is* meant to be shared, and performed. The process of preparing music for performance does contribute to the development of musical skill, and I believe is a necessary part of the learning process. But perhaps teachers and students should begin to rethink their priorities in structuring performance opportunities, and in setting their tone. When audiences and performers are in close contact with one another, it doesn't hurt the music one bit.

Obviously, our concert and recital traditions (as well as audience expectations) are going to be with us for a long time to come. When the setting is formal, the musician will simply have to use all the resources at his command to see that the music reaches, and moves, those who are present. In those traditions where music has openly mystical connotations, the artist does this by ensuring that he himself is the first among those present reached and moved by the music.

Notes

1. Virgil Thompson, "Music Does Not Flow," *The New York Review of Books,* December 17, 1981, p. 46.

2. Quoted in Harold Schonberg, *The Lives of the Great Composers,* Chapter 12 (Franz Liszt: Virtuoso, Charlatan—and Prophet), Norton, 1970, p. 182.

3. Eloise Ristad, *A Soprano on Her Head: Right Side Up Reflections on Life and Other Performances,* Real People Press, 1982.

4. Jack Meehan, "The Joy of Success," *The Instrumentalist,* November 1984, pp. 66–68.

11

If at First You Don't Succeed, Be Grateful

RANDOM THOUGHTS ABOUT STUDENT LIFE

Since I am not a music teacher, and this is not an instruction book, I owe you an explanation about its concluding chapter. We have now looked in great detail at some of the elements of the neuromuscular/audiovisual/biomechanical apparatus brought into play when you pick up your flute with something in mind beyond blowing bubbles or beaning your neighbor's poodle with it. I indicated at the outset that I hoped you would find this information enriching and possibly enlightening, but I couldn't promise you that it would be useful.

It would be serious misconduct for me to suggest that I have any tricks up my sleeve that might help you master the cello or the double bassoon. Even if I tried to sell you that line, you'd have to be pretty gullible to fall for it. After all, I began studying the piano for the first time just a few years ago—how much could I have learned in that time? Besides, you haven't even heard me play; if you *did* . . . well, never mind about that.

Notwithstanding the above, in case you have come to this point in the book with your appetite for music-making intact, there are a few thoughts I would like to share with you on the subject of music study. These have to do with pathfinding and pathkeeping—establishing a workable plan for yourself, then keeping your bearings in a landscape rich in ideas and helpful people. It is easy enough to want to get started; it is important to make provisions for the long haul.

Music is, or certainly should be, the shining example of recreational learning. You can start in the womb with marimba familiarization training and have yourself carted into a nursing home at age ninety-seven with bells lashed to the stretcher, hammering away at your favorite transcription of Beethoven's 24th Piano Sonata. Not only that: The scope of music is nothing less than oceanic. You can dampen your toe or head for 20,000 leagues. The manner, intensity, and longevity of the relationship is up to you.

Still, abundant though the enthusiasm of the musician may be, it is ridiculously easy to squelch. Any paradise can turn bleak, and anything we love is hiding its teeth. There is no other way to account for the number of musicians (some highly accomplished) who have given up their instruments. Inasmuch as I have offered encouragement so freely in these chapters, it seems not merely fair but *essential* that we examine the dropout problem. Forewarned is forearmed, I hope.

If you are at all like the average person, you took music lessons when you were young. You may have played in a school band or orchestra. You understood enough to do what was asked of you, but never really got the hang of it and then just quit. If you're over forty, the chances are good that you took lessons again for a few months sometime within the past ten years, made a little headway, then gave it up because there wasn't enough time and you weren't really getting anywhere. "Too bad, though," you said to yourself. "I sort of enjoyed it."

As duly noted above, even those with considerable experience and proven ability as musicians are often found on the sidelines. If such people tend to lose interest in music, we cannot cite its inherent complexity as the reason adults choose other activities for their recreational time, or have difficulty sustaining their enthusiasm. What becomes of people's interest in music-making? Why is it like a love affair that is either on (and passionate) or over? The recreational runner goes through phases, enthusiasm rising and falling, but is usually ready almost anytime to do a few laps, nice and easy. The musician is either working hard or has given it up.

I am convinced that the reason is *goals*. Somehow the idea has gotten into people's heads that the point of music-making is to perform pieces. I mean this in a special way: I mean that the object seems to be to have a repertoire, like a collection of trophies intended for display. When this is the case, music study can hardly be a form of play, entered into for relaxation, exploration, and fun. Instead, it becomes a laborious procedure for acquiring batches of notes, from first measure to last. Practice is undertaken to get the notes right as quickly as possible, and is dominated by the concern for avoiding mistakes, for getting a product in shape. So construed, practice is the price you pay to get where you're going. The smiles will come when people gather to admire the trophies.

In other words, we do not usually consider the training process itself worthy of our affection. We recognize that it's fun (even if it is also work) to practice a serve, or jog for a few miles on a country road. But it goes against the grain to embrace music practice as exciting or rewarding in itself. Since we cannot imagine this attitude in ourselves, we do nothing to cultivate it.

As with all forms of learning, time, interest, and a willingness to work are required. Beginners tend to resent the learning process, as though it were some sort of obstacle in their way, or a barrier to the success they hope to achieve. This impatience probably accounts for most of the failures that occur in music education. If beginning students (and perhaps advanced students as well) knew more about the natural pace of developing musical skills, they would fret a little less about their progress. More than this, though, the musician should feel that working at music is a joy in itself no matter what the ultimate goal, and in fact is the *real* reward. That's why it is never too late to begin.

We should now turn our attention to the matter of getting started. One of the truly remarkable things about this whole enterprise is the wealth of teaching material that is available to you. Your teacher can, and will, supply you with method books, technical exercises and scales, and music which has been carefully selected for its suitability to your particular stage of advancement. There are countless supplementary texts on music theory, improvisation, musical analysis, interpretation, style of play, and so on. There are even computer-based learning programs now in use, and more to come. The mass of this material is such, in fact, that it is almost impossible not to feel from the outset that you will never be able to penetrate the mysteries or fathom the complexities that confront you.

Since you have to start somewhere, I would like to suggest that you start by thinking about music-making as a physical discipline, and that you use this concept as your St. Christopher's medal, to safeguard your determination, your investment, your sense of humor, and your sanity as you venture further into terra incognita.

This piece of advice is neither original nor new; as I pointed out in an earlier chapter, Ortmann's book on the physiology of piano technique was published over fifty years ago, and a number of similarly oriented texts have been published since then. But the voices of these teachers have been given little notice until quite recently. Teaching professionals may stress musical concepts (i.e., chord structure, rhythm, phrasing, and so forth) to their students, considering physical concepts, or "technique," to be merely a necessary (and boring) evil.

Perhaps we should take a close look at the word *technique;* the term has connotations which are both negative and limiting, and certainly falls far short of describing what I think of as the physical discipline involved in musical skill.

When I began music lessons, I learned that "technique" was a segregated and obligatory part of each day's practice schedule, devoted to playing scales, arpeggios, and finger exercises. I wouldn't blame my teacher for my negative feelings about this work, but it was like paying dues; you had to do a certain amount of this stuff to get your fingers to behave. It was only after I had been doing this for a while that I began to notice how often the music critics badger performing artists about the mechanical aspects of their play—either the musician lacked "technique" (was just plain clumsy) or was not worth listening to because the playing was "nothing more than technique—all the right notes but no music."

Herbert Whone, the violinist, has written a thoughtful and provocative article on this matter, which he called "Technique—A Dangerous Concept." He poses the issue this way:

> How is it that some players convey a sense of fulfillment, and others one of imbalance and inadequacy? Some, whether through an innate or an acquired balance of their faculties, are able to transcend any sense of struggle and become a vehicle for something other than themselves. This causes us to experience that marvelous sense of effortless play in a performance.[1]

This makes sense; if technique just means digital dexterity, I think it's a waste of time. On the other hand, "an innate or acquired balance of the faculties" represents something worth striving for. It brings to mind a fundamental tenet of Zen thought, which holds that one studies flower arranging, or archery, or motorcycle maintenance, for only one reason: to achieve detachment through self-mastery. Perhaps this formulation is as good a bridge to the deeper levels of musical meaning, and the value of music as a discipline, as can be found. It allows us to see that the spiritual, cerebral, and physical aspects of music are not only unopposed but in fact mutually dependent. And, to be very practical, it gives us a solid foundation on which to anchor our interest in music-making, and from which to build a long-range, workable plan for both success and satisfaction.

Early in the book it was proposed that the musician is an athlete who has specialized the use of his own small muscles to control the production of sound from a musical instrument. Consistent with this view would be a training program which takes account of the special nature of these muscles and their control apparatus. Thus, an early goal must be to gain facility with the basic movements needed to coax sound from an instrument; the next step is to learn to connect sequences of such movements to a musical plan, whether written or improvised. The next objective is to bring these movements under the control of the auditory system—ideally, you begin to learn how to play an instrument and music simultaneously, and from the beginning are training the ear to control the whole process. The overriding objective is to develop fluency in a musical language, and the competence to use that language to speak in a voice that would otherwise be silent. One gets caught up in the complexity of the material of music so quickly that it is easy to miss the emergence of this new mode of communication, or to neglect its cultivation; it is also easy to forget the aspect of self-discovery which occurs through the effort to become expert in a special physical skill.

Another way to lose sight of the physical side of music-making is by having a teacher who is so drawn to the aesthetics of music that the mechanics never become a subject of serious analysis. There is nothing inherently wrong with such an approach, I am sure, but some of us need lots of help getting past the feeling we're trying to play with boxing gloves. I, for one, happen to think things go more smoothly if you never lose sight of the interaction of musical and physical ideas.

This brings us to a fascinating issue, which might make for

an interesting psychosociological research project, maybe even a book: how to select, retain, and/or change a music teacher. Probably no single decision you make will have a greater impact on the outcome of your musical aspirations, and probably no single decision in a musician's life is made so naively.

It would be easy enough to say that there is a range of teachers from sublime to criminally bad (as with all the other professions), but this observation would hardly provide you with much insight into the situation, or equip you to make the right choice. What you need to know is something about how teachers approach their work and their students, and what your contribution to the relationship has to be if it is to succeed.

Music teaching luxuriates in a climate of fragmented goals and methods. Music itself defies definition, and therefore frustrates any attempt to prescribe the skills of its practitioners. Music students, moreover, are such an independent breed that *any* proposal for a codified pedagogy tends to meet with indifference (or derision) from experienced teachers. A professionally standardized, objectively validated, and universally applied curriculum for instrumental or vocal study has been neither a practical necessity nor a practical possibility. The earnest and hardworking music teacher devises a personal approach, preserving whatever succeeds and dropping whatever does not, and the gifted student does the same.

In practical terms, this means you have to do a little research before you sign up for lessons; otherwise you may be surprised to encounter a teaching situation which simply does not work. What kind of research? First, having gleaned what you can from the grapevine, discuss your interest in music with several teachers. Explore their approach, and their specific musical interests. Find out how they feel about the teaching of musical analysis—sight reading, music theory, and harmony, or ear training, for example. Do they teach composition, or improvisation? What is their approach to technical training? This must be an area of major concern for anyone with serious interest in skilled playing; when it is ignored or badly taught, the consequences can be disastrous, as we shall see. Finally, do they feel it is valuable to perform, and do they offer student recitals or master classes? You may not *want* all of this but you should find out what is available, and how it is taught if it is of interest to you.

Discussing these topics with more than one teacher might help you peg the teacher with whom you could best work at close quarters. Don't hesitate to interview some of a teacher's other students.

Second, agree with your new teacher that you will take your first few lessons on a trial basis. Decide ahead of time what you expect to have accomplished in five or ten lessons and agree that you will sit down together at the end of that period to take stock. If either of you suspects the arrangement won't work out, you can part company as friends. That's hard to do if you wait too long.

Suppose you did your homework, but find things are not working as you had supposed they would, and you are beginning to regret your choice. Given the spirited state of consumerism in this country, one would suppose that such a situation would correct itself. It is not so easy to tell your teacher that he or she is not living up to expectations. The beginning music student, however determined, is easily overwhelmed, and inclined to be guilt-ridden when things do not go well. If expectations are not being met, the student and teacher may both conclude that the student has no talent, and both will agree that the student should throw in the towel. Usually such a student is unwilling to risk humiliation again anytime soon.

When things are not going well, it is rarely the *method* that is called into question. On what grounds could the beginning student make such a judgment? This point is made not as a criticism of music teachers but as a reminder that teacher and student, with the best intentions, may unwittingly and jointly collaborate in a needless failure. When this happens it is the student who bears the psychological brunt of the failure.

There is another area of potential difficulty, much less likely to occur but far more difficult to deal with than the problem we have just looked at. Suppose things work out well, and you are satisfied your teacher was made in heaven. As you gain skill and learn more about music, you may find you want to take a stronger hand in your own development. There may be a particular work you want to tackle, or a style of play you feel you should explore. This is a point in your upbringing with explosive potential. Music teachers, bless them, love their work and their students, and generally have strong opinions about what is best. Their pride in their work may be so strong, however, that they will show you the door if you do not do things their way. I am awestruck when principles are held with this much conviction, but personally prefer to be free to enjoy the fruits of my own dumb decisions.

Inevitably, the longer you stay with one teacher, the greater the likelihood you and your teacher will differ on a matter of importance. Because of the closeness of the relationship between teacher and student in music, a major disagreement can cause extraordinary anguish to both.

Without realizing it, you invest your teacher with enormous power. The teacher tells you what to do, explains to you how to do it, and then tells you whether you did it well or not. If you are running in a ten kilometer race, you can look at your own stopwatch, review your previous times, and decide how well you are doing. You can play through any piece you are studying and know whether or not you got the notes in the right order. But that's not the issue: The issue is, how did it sound? Did you make music? Did you communicate? In my view, your training must from the very beginning deliberately guide you toward the goal of making your own independent judgments about the quality of your playing. There is a serious threat to your growth if this does not occur, because if your interpretation must always be approved by someone with greater knowledge, your music ultimately can only be imitative. If this happens, you've missed the boat.

Let us return briefly to the matter of the teacher's approach to "technique." I asserted that inattention to this issue could have disastrous consequences; this is so because musicians, like football and hockey players, sometimes get injured in the line of duty, and your "coach" should know how to keep you out of the infirmary.

In the past few years the public has learned of the tragic interruption of the careers of several notable concert artists because of disabling pain, numbness, or weakness in an arm or hand. It was not until the reports of these problems had widely circulated that physicians began hearing from musician-patients that they, too, were in pain when they played. These disclosures quickly gave rise to the novel and unexpected impression that the musical career is not without physical peril. Two things are abundantly clear: First, physical complaints *specifically related to practice technique* are widespread among musicians; second, the musicians with such complaints rarely bring them to the attention of their teachers or health professionals. Either it does not occur to them that pain is abnormal or they fear the harmful consequences to their careers of a "confession" of such problems.

The problem is of real importance. Dorothy Taubman, a piano teacher in New York who has made pianists' injuries a special interest for a number of years, declares that faulty piano technique is virtually always responsible for these injuries, and that the whole subject is badly in need of careful scrutiny and open discussion by music educators.[2] She is presently working on her own book, but in the meantime offers this advice: "When movements are correctly executed, the feeling is delicious. If it hurts, you're injuring yourself and you need to find another way to do it!" This advice applies to violinists, drummers, guitarists, and harpists as well as to pianists. Mrs. Taubman seems to be saying that good technique not only serves the artist's musical goals, it has the same effect as eating an apple a day. I'm sold.

Some of the stories of musicians' physical problems are actually quite funny, until you consider what they say about the guarded communications between some students and their teachers. I recall a discussion several years ago in a group that included a very successful young pianist and his teacher of twelve years. The topic was stage fright. The young man described with considerable humor his own problems with nerves, which had finally settled into a practice of ritual (usually fake) vomiting before performances. His teacher was dumbfounded: In twelve years of intense work with his star pupil, this was the first time he had heard of the problem.* If there were any remaining doubt that musical study can produce injury, one need only take notice of the signs that a new field of medicine is emerging to deal with such problems.[3 4 5]

The take-home lesson for you, as a beginner, is this: Music is a healthful activity. It is good for you. So is running. But you can sprain your knee or your ankle by running incorrectly, and with a faulty technique you can do the same thing to your hand playing the guitar, the piano, or almost anything else. Don't ignore pain if it develops. If your teacher says it doesn't matter,

*When I first related this story to a friend who spends a lot of his time with professional musicians, he laughed. "That's really quite common," he said. "In fact, there's a joke about it. Just before the start of an opera, the stage manager rushes into the diva's dressing room and blurts out, 'Madame, the conductor's plane had to go to another airport and he can't get here on time. The program has been canceled.' She looks at the man in shock and says: 'But it is *impossible!* You cannot cancel; I have already thrown up!' "

or something cheery like "no pain, no gain," in my humble opinion you are entitled to a refund and should take your dreams and your business elsewhere.

Before moving on, I want to summarize the intent of all this. You would not start music unless you were eager to work. Music teachers abound, and are ready to help. You owe it to yourself, and to your teacher, to make several decisions at the beginning carefully: What kind of instrument do you want to learn to play; what kind of music would you like to be able to play; what kind of teaching is available; who seems to be the best teacher for you?

Having made this much of a good start, make sure you and your teacher have a collaborative relationship. Ask questions, don't hide your problems, and don't sacrifice your own enthusiasm to save the teacher's feelings. If you don't like the way things are going, speak up. Finally, make sure you are doing everything possible to increase your understanding of musical structure: Go to concerts; buy records; talk about your music with your teacher and other students. Bite the bullet and learn something about music theory. Try composing; get into an ensemble; take a class in improvisation. All of this will contribute to the full development of your potential and to your satisfaction while you study.

At its worst, music teaching begins with a threat ("Be back here next week with the C major scale in two hands") and continues as an ego-bruising succession of encounters devoted to correcting mistakes. At its best, it offers an open door to yourself and to life that will take you anywhere you want it to.

WARNING!

PAY NO ATTENTION TO THE FOLLOWING

Having declared myself unqualified to say anything specific or practical about study, and with appropriate disclaimers, I would like to indulge in some highly speculative thinking about the advantages of a physical mind-set in music study. My reason for doing this is I think you will make your way in music much more happily if you develop, and then use, your own perceptions as the guide. You cannot and will not succeed without a good teacher. But every good teacher I've met always said essentially the same thing: In the final analysis, we do nothing more than make it possible for the student to teach himself or herself. I admire the modesty, and absolutely agree with the sentiment.

How can you contribute to your own development as a self-teacher? In its generic form the question is, how do you learn to trust your own judgment? The answer is, by doing everything you can to sharpen your eyes and ears. And how do you sharpen your eyes and ears? The answer is, by learning how to do something difficult. If this sounds like a circle, you have an excellent short-term memory. All I said was this: Learning teaches you to learn. Since learning requires you to see and hear clearly and accurately, your progress will prove to you that you can believe your own eyes and ears. And you should come to trust yourself. This is the goal of education, if you want my opinion. Now, off the mountaintop and into the learning lab.

Educational psychologists tell us that we learn to improve motor skills because of what is termed "knowledge of results."[6] We start out with some sort of mental representation of what we want to accomplish. We formulate a physical strategy, based on previous experience with similar or somehow comparable tasks, to achieve the results we desire. We execute the plan and note the outcome. Even with very unfamiliar tasks (such as playing a musical instrument, if we've never done this before) we can usually tell how close we came to the desired result, and what needs to be fixed if we're going to do better next time.

It is worth pausing a moment to reflect on this particular aspect of our natural learning ability. When we decide we want to learn how to do something new, we have a reasonably good idea of what our goal is, and can usually formulate at least a rough estimate of what must be changed if we are to meet that goal. This is true even if we are not completely sure of the steps that must be taken to make the desired change. Suppose that we were equipped to judge only *absolute* success or failure as we attempt to acquire a new skill. For example, suppose we decided to try to learn to throw a basketball though a hoop, but had no way of knowing anything about the results of our attempts except whether the ball went through the hoop or not. One way to simulate this situation would be to put on a blindfold and wear earplugs and ask someone to tap us on the shoulder whenever we hit the target. How long do you think it would be before you would get the ball through the hoop, how likely is it that you would be able to reproduce your performance if you *did* score, and how long do you think you would find this an interesting thing to do?

Of course, we would not be likely to waste much time on a learning situation like this, because experience tells us that our efforts would be futile. And the reason they would be futile is that we learn by small steps and successive approximations; we have the capacity to appreciate the size and direction of errors we make, and to use that information to modify our performance so that we can continue to narrow the gap between the current and the desired level of proficiency. If we were not able to detect, analyze, and build on *partial* success, we would never know how to make the changes needed to bring us to a goal we have set for ourselves.

This brings us to a fascinating paradox. Since learning is a process intended to produce change, it is essential that we learn to embrace our errors, indeed to treasure them and rejoice in them, rather than deny or despair in them. For it is our *mistakes*, when we understand them, that instruct us.

As you venture into the world of music in order to refine your own motor skills, remember the paradox, and take heart in your own tendency to improve at a snail's pace: Our physiologic makeup ordains us for a process of change and improvement that will take place in steps. As we discussed in the chapter on the motor control system, it is because of this arrangement that improvement becomes stable and dependable. As students, we are poor learners if embarrassed or angered by our errors and impatient for progress; unless advancement proceeds on a base of well-planned and closely observed change, it will be short-lived and limited.

Educational theorists have considered that there may be times when it is appropriate to learn by making mistakes and correcting them (the discovery method), and times to proceed very slowly, only after the exact steps are known and can be executed in an error-free manner.[7] It is an interesting debate, and it leads us into one of the few issues in music where current knowledge appears to justify the attempt to use a physiologic argument in support of pedagogic principle.

Isidor Philipp, the great piano teacher, wrote about practicing while he was at the Paris Conservatory, and said this about speed: "Too much stress cannot be laid upon the usefulness, the necessity of *slow work.* The greatest masters agree on this. Stephen Heller gave me a rather striking motto—'Practice very slowly—progress very fast,' and Saint-Saëns also said, in the humorous way he had of expressing himself: 'One must practice slowly, then more slowly and finally slowly.' "[8]

Rosario Mazzeo, whom I mentioned briefly in reference to the photographer Ansel Adams, is a woodwind teacher who by reputation is without peer. In his book on the clarinet he explains this point about study simply and elegantly: "Studying is more concerned with examination of a problem, and 'practicing' with repetition of certain motions or actions, to make them a habit.

Therefore one's first thought (when faced with a passage not mastered) should be *not* to practice it. If you do, you will only make a habit of the errors as assiduously as you do the parts you *can* play. . . ."[9]

Confirmation of these teaching precepts comes from the work of motor system physiologists, in my opinion. During the early stages of learning and memorization of a music work (and I am not speaking only of works for the piano) one is engaged in a process of automatizing certain aspects of a sequence of carefully ordered discrete movements; this is what must be done if they are to be made ballistic—capable of being performed at the appropriate tempo in an error-free manner. The evidence now seems very compelling that the musician is at this stage engaged in developing a stored memory of these sequences within the motor system in its entirety. That memory includes the order of contractions, and a superimposed, highly ordered series of relaxations to surround and facilitate the contractions. It includes adaptive postural movements of the entire skeletal system which will form a background of support for the orientation of the small muscles in relation to the instrument. It includes specific details of the proportional relationships of movements in time, individually and in relation to one another.

Two things can be said about the process that would seem to validate what Philipp, Mazzeo, and others say about practicing. First, whatever is automatic in the movement sequence becomes established through repetitions that are executed with consistency. If practicing takes place at a pace too fast for accurate execution, the musician will end up with more than one version of the performance, any one of which may present itself in public according to whim. The second thing about the process that can be said is that done properly, it really does produce reliable performance; practice one version faithfully and that's the one you will have for the stage. Therefore, it is probably wise to refrain from practice (in the sense Mazzeo uses the word) until you are satisfied that you know how you want the finished product to sound. Failure to heed this warning will place you in the company of the unhappy swarms of tennis players and golfers struggling to change a stroke or a swing that was learned incorrectly. The motor system will do its programming job efficiently and durably, with the result that bad habits and good habits become equally difficult to eradicate.

There has already been ample discussion of the negative effects of compulsive worry over mistakes. The human neuromuscular system is a machine, but it is not a machine. It will do what you ask of it, to the best of its ability, and give you more than you ask most of the time. Electronic synthesizers under the control of computers are capable of precise and highly reproducible performance, and are thought by some to be the ideal replacement for human musicians. However, I see little danger that audiences will prefer machines to live performers until engineers can get the things to be both precise and *un*predictable.

How is the student to strike a balance? What is the point of killing yourself to get the notes right if accuracy isn't the ultimate purpose of the exercise? What *is* the purpose?

This time there is only silence from the mountaintop. You can strive for anything you want to. You can try to play like Heifetz, and remind yourself to make at least *one* mistake before you go to bed each night, or work to become the ultimate improviser, never playing anything the same way twice. None of it will ever be perfect. Even if it is, there will be another way to do it.

So you might as well relax and play!

Notes

1. Herbert Whone, " 'Technique'—A Dangerous Concept," *Strad,* June 1982, p. 106.

2. Audrey Schneider, "Dorothy Taubman: 'There is an Answer,' " *Clavier,* September 1983, pp. 19–21.

3. Terra Ziporyn, "Pianist's Cramp to Stage Fright: The Medical Side of Music-Making," *Journal of the American Medical Association,* August 24/31, 1984, pp. 985–989.

4. Christine Hinz, "MDs Meet Musicians' Medical Needs," *American Medical News,* August 17, 1984, pp. 1–27.

5. Amity Shlaes, "Performing Artists Hear Different Tune from Medicine Now," *Wall Street Journal,* December 6, 1984, p. 1.

6. Karl Newell, "Skill Learning," in *Human Skills: Studies in Human Performance,* Chapter 9, ed. D. Holding, Wiley, 1981, pp. 203–227.

7. Robert Singer, "To Err or Not to Err: A Question for the Instruction of Psychomotor Skills," *Review of Educational Research,* Summer 1977, pp. 479–498.

8. Isidor Philipp, *Some Reflections on Piano Playing,* Durand & Cie., 1928. Reprinted in *The Piano Quarterly,* #88, Winter 1974–75.

9. Rosario Mazzeo, *The Clarinet: Excellence and Artistry,* Alfred Publishing, 1981, p. 2.

Coda

I have sought primarily to do four things: first, to lend credibility to the notion that music-making is a physical skill; second, to explain certain essential differences between music-making and athletic skills, linking music with human creativity and language; third, to draw parallels between the learning of traditional athletic skills and those involved in music-making; finally, to suggest that music learning (as with other skills) proceeds most efficiently and happily, and goes further, when the student is encouraged to become an objective and thoughtful observer of his or her own development.

I decided to write this book because of my own experience as an adult beginner, and also because of feelings I have as a parent, a physician, and an admirer of Auntie Mame. If I have succeeded, you will have come a little closer to your own personal musicality, either as a music-maker or as a devoted music lover.

Music, as an experience, is certainly one of life's great treasures. It did not occur to me until I began my own studies that the great joy of listening to music arises in the most unexpected, delightful, and profound ways once you have had personal experience with its creation. As my own experience increased, so did my awareness of the elegance and subtlety of the music of those I was listening to. My own efforts at music-making may have been clumsy, but they were earnest, and rewarded me with a far less passive set of ears and eyes; I become more and more closely drawn into the act of creation—the dance of sight and sound—that occurs whenever any musician presents his or her work to others.

The more I thought about the transformation of my own responses, the more irritated I became at my own lifelong unquestioning acceptance of the exclusiveness of music-making. I understand and fully accept the necessity for a high standard in the public performance of music, and don't begrudge the pedestal society erects for our most gifted musicians. We really do need to protect and preserve the expressive potential of great music. But if our deference to musical excellence obliges us repress or deny the humble musicality of those unqualified for a place on the pedestal, then I'm against it. Music-making doesn't just belong to people with talent; by biologic heritage it belongs to everyone. I certainly don't expect all the musicians to agree with this thesis, but some will, and perhaps the late bloomers and nonprodigies will be taken more seriously by teaching professionals. That would help.

My secondary purpose has been to make explicit certain aspects of the special relationship between the brain and music. Of the many provocative and poetic statements on this theme, my favorite is that of Dr. Lewis Thomas (in *The Medusa and the Snail,* Viking Penguin, 1979). In his famous essay "On Thinking About Thinking," he writes:

> Instead of using what we can guess at about the nature of thought to explain the nature of music, start over again. Begin with music and see what it can tell us about the sensation of thinking. Music is the effort we make to explain to ourselves how our brains work. . . . If you want, as an experiment, to hear the whole mind working, all at once, put on the *St. Matthew Passion* and turn the volume up all the way. That is the sound of the whole central nervous system of human beings, all at once.

This book will have succeeded completely if it draws attention to the growing dialogue on human musicality among educators, musicians, and medical and behavioral scientists. We need to know more about the physical creation of music, and how to open that experience to more people. We need more information about how musical skills are acquired by people whether they *are* or *aren't* prodigies, at whatever age. We need to find out whether active music-making really contributes to cognitive and emotional development in children, whether it could be effectively used to prevent or mitigate some of the forms of senility which afflict older people, and how it might be employed in the treatment of those with injury to the neuromuscular system. These are not simple questions.

Lastly, we all need to remember to have fun, and I think I will have succeeded if a few folks decide to take a crack at the banjo, the trombone, or even the bagpipes, just for a lark.

November 18, 1982

Dr. Wilson:

Thanks for your views, as picked up by AP and in the enclosed Orange County *Register*.

Thoroughly enjoyed reading your opinions, which my personal experience fully support. As a sixty-two-year-old, third-year early-retiree, I started taking bagpipe lessons this past spring. It's great, even learning alongside thirteen-year-olds!

Your words are especially encouraging to those of us in the fogey class.

Appreciatively,
Mac McRobbie

ABOUT THE AUTHOR

Frank R. Wilson, M.D., is Assistant Clinical Professor of Neurology at San Francisco's University of California Medical Center and he lectures frequently on the neurological basis of music-making. He was recognized at an early age by his parents and teachers as a musical non-prodigy. After studying piano for only three months in junior high school he was urged to try the bass drum. He found this instrument too heavy to carry, so he took up the snare drum, and joined a marching band. Once, during high school, he tried to play the French horn, but was unable to produce a sound from it within the range of human hearing. During his college, Navy, and medical school years, he owned a harmonica, but he never played it. After becoming a neurologist, he found he was insanely jealous of his two musical children, and vowed to mortify them by returning to the piano, his first love. Both children have moved away from home and now support themselves.